Beyond the Left:
The Communist
Critique of
the Media

Beyond the Left:
The Communist Critique of the Media

Stephen Harper

Winchester, UK
Washington, USA

First published by Zero Books, 2012
Zero Books is an imprint of John Hunt Publishing Ltd., Laurel House, Station Approach,
Alresford, Hants, SO24 9JH, UK
office1@o-books.net
www.o-books.com

For distributor details and how to order please visit the 'Ordering' section on our website.

Text copyright: Stephen Harper 2010

ISBN: 978 1 84694 976 0

A CIP catalogue record for this book is available from the British Library.

Design: Stuart Davies

Printed in the UK by CPI Antony Rowe
Printed in the USA by Offset Paperback Mfrs, Inc

We operate a distinctive and ethical publishing philosophy in all
areas of our business, from our global network of authors to
production and worldwide distribution.

CONTENTS

Introduction: to bind and guide the world

> It remains a fact that in almost every act of our daily lives, whether in the sphere of politics or business, in our social conduct or our ethical thinking, we are dominated by a relatively small number of persons [...] who understand the mental processes and social patterns of the masses. It is they who pull the wires which control the public mind, who harness old social forces and contrive new ways to bind and guide the world – Edward Bernays, *Propaganda* (1928)

The century since the American 'father of Public Relations', Edward Bernays, penned these words has been marked by stupendous advances in media and communications technology. Yet the unequal social relations which Bernays describes – and to whose furtherance Bernays dedicated his career as a US state and corporate propagandist – still pertain. *Propaganda* constituted a direct response to the socio-economic impasses of US capitalism in the 1920s, as a dearth of new markets, a crisis of overproduction and the lingering menace of proletarian revolution forced capitalists to devise ever more ingenious methods of mass persuasion; yet its account of a technocratic elite of mind managers that manipulates and regulates public opinion in the interests of the ruling class remains more relevant than ever. This book presents an overview of the ideological machinations of the contemporary news and current affairs media, written from a communist perspective – that is, from the perspective not of an unchanging set of ideas, but of what Karl Marx and Friedrich Engels, in *The German Ideology*, called the 'real movement that abolishes the present state of things'. Beleaguered and unstable as it is, the capitalist system continues to reproduce our social world – a world characterised by war, starvation, poverty and environmental destruction. Yet today, as in Bernays' era, there exists another force in society – the working class – that from a communist perspective provides the only hope 'to bind and guide the world' towards a human future. This book identifies and critiques some of the ideological messages communicated by what Bernays called the 'wires which control the public mind' – in particular the news and current affairs media – in the context of the political, social and cultural struggle between the ruling class and the working class.

In the present conjuncture, starting a book by invoking class struggle politics may seem imprudent. As an approach to understanding and acting upon the world, communism is distinctly unfashionable: it is possible that more people today believe in aliens or homeopathy than in the desirability of a global working class revolution. This state of affairs is hardly surprising. Despite the increasingly apparent economic instability at the heart of the system, the ideologues of capitalism stubbornly maintain, in tones ranging from resigned to triumphant, that capitalism reigns supreme – or at least that, to quote Margaret Thatcher, 'There Is No Alternative' to the current mode of production. As Francis Fukuyama boldly asserted following the collapse of the Soviet Union in his book *The End of History*, 'liberal democracy in reality constitutes the best possible solution to the human problem'. In the face of this wretched consensus, it can appear that we are now 'living without an alternative', in Zygmunt Bauman's famous phrase. In the past, economists such as Keynes routinely discussed when the capitalist mode of production would come to an end; yet today's economists – whether out of embarrassment, fear or denial – tend not to raise this question. In the cultural imaginary, too, alternatives to capitalism are seldom posited; thus Slavoj Žižek endorses Fredric Jameson's observation that it is now easier for us to imagine the final destruction of human species – a scenario worked through in myriad Hollywood apocalypse films – than it is to envisage a change in the way human society is organised.

At first glance, the prospect of abolishing the class system through a radical re-organisation of global production – the process and results of which are known to Marxists and anarchists as communism – does indeed look remote. In Britain, as elsewhere, the working class is only just rediscovering its sense of confidence and militancy after the bitter experiences of the 1980s – notably, the state's defeat of the Miners' Strike. Politicians assure the public that everybody is now middle class, while relatively few proletarians self-identify as working class or engage in radical politics. In the universities, too, communism has receded as an explanatory and analytical paradigm: academic research is increasingly funded and conducted according to a business model, as the flawed but indulgent concept of liberal education gives way to market forces and the deadening jargon of 'employability' and 'skills'. Yet try as they might, the forces of capitalism cannot dispel their nemesis, communism – and they cannot stop workers from struggling to forge the human future that communism represents. Despite the scandalous arrogation of the adjectives 'Marxist', 'communist' and 'socialist' by capitalist states past and present – from the Soviet Union to Venezuela – and despite the perpetuation of such falsifications by a host of academics and journalists, communism remains a revolutionary force across the world, as working class militancy grows in response to the global crisis of capitalism. Marxian theory, meanwhile, remains the most powerful paradigm for understanding both capitalism and the products of its media industries. But Marxism is an almost forgotten critical paradigm within the field of critical media studies today. Indeed, this book's titular promise to outline 'the' communist critique of the media derives less from a desire to claim this short text as definitive than from a feeling that communist perspectives are widely misunderstood or neglected in contemporary critical circles and that their fundamental elements and insights therefore need to be restated.

Without doubt, capitalism has been the most dynamic mode of production the world has ever known; Marx himself marvelled at its achievements. Yet capitalist social relations, in Marxian jargon, ultimately become a fetter on the development of humanity's productive forces. The massive and relentless destruction of human life and infrastructure in the last one hundred years indicates that capitalism is less and less able to realise its gains in productivity at the social level. The workers' movement of a century ago recognised what is today so often overlooked or denied: that capitalism, wracked by its internal contradictions, had undergone a decisive shift and had entered a period of decay. Having abolished scarcity and made communism possible by the early twentieth century, capitalism today is an obsolete system whose continuance offers humanity only increasing misery. As the social symptoms of this retrogression – poverty, starvation, holocausts, environmental degradation and economies increasingly based upon drugs, arms and gangsterism – become more difficult to disguise, the media play a vital role, it is argued here, in concealing their systemic origins.

Based on a number of short case studies, this book analyses how the capitalist media uphold the capitalist *status quo* and emphasize the necessity of exploitation, nationalism and imperialism. But it is imperative to realise that the ideological orientation of the capitalist media is not only, or even primarily, right-wing. Indeed, in keeping with the principles of communist politics, this book critiques not just the stratagems of the conservative press and broadcasters, but also the ideological subterfuges of the 'progressive' media. A key argument of the book is that journalists and the left-liberal commentariat – in their advocacy of such shibboleths as 'humanitarian intervention', 'national defence', 'green politics' and 'anti-fascism' – play an even more insidious role in the ideological justification of capitalist social relations than the system's right-wing apologists. This is especially true in so-called 'advanced' capitalist countries such as the United Kingdom, whose news media constitute the principal focus of this critique. There is no space in this short text to discuss in detail questions of news media institutions, the working practices of journalists, or the ways in which media audiences interact with the news media; yet these omissions do not in themselves invalidate the book's arguments, which focus primarily on ideological messages and meanings.

As well as identifying and contesting the propaganda of the capitalist media, this book challenges a wide range of academic and journalistic opinion about politics and the media. Since academics and journalists are seldom favourably disposed towards communism, the tone of this book is rarely peaceable. Undoubtedly, too, many liberals will find the book 'biased'; after all, as Michael Parenti succinctly notes in *Inventing Reality*, 'people who never complain about the one-sidedness of their mainstream political education are the first to complain of the one-sidedness of any challenge to it'. But as capitalism drags humanity towards annihilation and the validity of Rosa Luxemburg's perspective of 'socialism or barbarism' becomes ever clearer, political neutrality is hardly an option. Here we can do no better than repeat Walter Benjamin's austere advice: 'anyone incapable of taking sides should say nothing'.

1

Different worlds: the ruling class and the working class

> The working class and the employing class have nothing in common – Preamble to the International Workers of the World constitution (1905)

As bell hooks notes at the start of her book *Where We Stand*, 'nowadays it is fashionable to talk about race or gender; the uncool subject is class. It's the subject that makes us all tense, nervous, uncertain about where we stand'. The contemporary queasiness about 'class' is reflected by the virtual eradication of the word from mainstream media discourse. News reports typically refer to 'ordinary' rather than working class people. Governments, too, increasingly forswear the language of class exploitation, preferring the more emollient rhetoric of 'marginalisation' and 'social exclusion' – keywords in what Pierre Bourdieu and Loïc Wacquant, in their article on 'neoliberal newspeak', have called the 'new planetary vulgate' of liberal capitalism, 'from which the terms "capitalism", "class", "exploitation", "domination", and "inequality" are conspicuous by their absence'. In academia, meanwhile, class has become what Ulrich Beck calls a 'zombie category' that continues to haunt critical discourse although its substantive content has largely been hollowed out. If we are to understand capitalism or its media from a communist perspective, however, class must be our starting point.

The theory and practice of communism are premised on the analysis of capitalism. In *The Communist Manifesto* of 1848, Marx and Engels proposed that capitalism was spreading across the globe and that the structure of industrialised societies was increasingly bifurcating into two mutually antagonistic classes. The bourgeoisie or ruling class owns the means of production (such as factories, supermarkets, schools or call centres) and derives profit from the 'surplus value' produced by workers. The proletariat or working class creates the society's wealth, producing commodities in return for a wage. The terms of this basic analysis remain relevant today. It is certainly true that many contemporary workers hold wrongheaded or confused opinions about the nature of their class interests. It is also true that deindustrialisation, gentrification, the breakdown of the extended family and many other factors have wrought massive changes in the nature of working class culture in Western countries in recent decades. It must also be acknowledged that some individuals occupy conflicted class positions that are resistant to classification; as Martin Glaberman notes in his pamphlet *The Working Class and Social Change*, the communist view of class, unlike its sociological counterpart, does not attempt to account for everybody and is no less valid for that. Yet as capitalism's crisis deepens, the fundamental fact of working class existence – exploitation – is more palpable than ever, as is the social antagonism between the exploited and their rulers. In fact, *The Communist Manifesto*'s description of class polarisation now seems grimly prescient: since Marx's era, when the global working class was massively outnumbered by the peasantry, capitalism has conquered the entire globe, subjecting ever greater swathes of humanity to its rule.

For communists, class – rather than gender, sexuality, race or nationality – is the central category of political and social analysis. In his 2008 *New Left Review* article 'Against diversity', Walter Benn Michaels bluntly proposes that American liberals tend to 'carry on about racism and sexism in order to avoid doing so about capitalism'. Michaels observes that decades of anti-racist and anti-sexist legislation and campaigning in the US, far from reducing inequality, have been perfectly compatible with its deepening:

> In 1947 – seven years before the Supreme Court decision in Brown v. Board of Education, sixteen years before the publication of Betty Friedan's *The Feminine Mystique* – the top fifth of American wage-earners made 43 per cent of the money earned in the US. Today that same quintile gets 50.5 per cent. In 1947, the bottom fifth of wage-earners got 5 per cent of total income; today it gets 3.4 per cent. After half a century of anti-racism and feminism, the US today is a less equal society than was the racist, sexist society of Jim Crow. Furthermore, virtually all the growth in inequality has taken place since the passage of the Civil Rights Act of 1965 – which means not only that the successes of the struggle against discrimination have failed to alleviate inequality, but that they have been compatible with a radical expansion of it. Indeed, they have helped to enable the increasing gulf between rich and poor.

When there is exploitation to be done, capitalism is essentially blind to differences of gender, race and sexuality. Although the cultivation of racism, sexism and homophobia often proves politically useful to capitalists, it is perfectly possible, in theory at least, for capitalism to offer formal equality to black people, women, and homosexuals. It follows that feminism, civil rights and gay rights movements do not in themselves threaten capitalism as class struggles do. The attempts of New Left theoreticians and contemporary hegemony theorists to posit the replacement of the working class as a revolutionary subject with a coalition of identity groups are therefore highly problematic. Unlike other categories of social difference, class constitutes an absolute division in capitalist society, since the antagonism between the exploited and exploiting classes is the system's essential structural feature.

Politicians naturally attempt to deny or mystify this antagonism through a variety of strategies. In so-called 'rich' states
such as Britain and the US, they have periodically propagated the
myth of a universal middle class. When Labour came to power in
the UK in 1997, for example, the party's John Prescott declared
the class struggle to be over, asserting that Britons were 'all
middle class'. Just a few years later, Tony Blair argued that the
working class was disappearing and giving way to 'an expanded
middle class, with ladders of opportunity for those of all
backgrounds'. Yet if anything, the 'middle class' of relatively
well-off workers has been shrinking since the 1970s, as
capitalism's economic crisis forces workers to work longer for
less pay and previously privileged groups of workers are prole-
tarianised.

When they are not denying the existence of the working class,
politicians seeking to boost their public credibility like to claim
membership of it. On the BBC's political discussion programme
The Andrew Marr Show (23 May 2010), for example, Labour's
Andy Burnham – a self-described socialist – professed his
frustration that too few people can access professions such as
politics, law and the media, frequently alluding to his own
working class 'background'. Similarly, in a BBC documentary
entitled *John Prescott: The Class System and Me* (2008), John
Prescott embarked on a quest to understand the meaning of class,
identifying himself as a worker, despite his erstwhile denial of
class hierarchies. Tucking into a portion of fish and chips,
Prescott averred that his unpretentious meal signalled his proletarian status and claimed that he draws strength from the
support he receives from 'ordinary working people'. 'They give
you that succour', said Prescott, 'that comfort that comes from
solidarity, even though they know I'm in a different kind of world
than they are'. Presenting himself as a man of the people, Prescott
distanced himself from the accusations of luxurious living that
once earned him the mocking soubriquet 'Two Jags'. Yet Prescott

does inhabit 'a different kind of world' to the working class people whom he claims support him. This is not just a question of his lifestyle choices. Communists understand class as a relation to the means of production, which one class owns and controls and another uses in production. No matter how many chips or pints of beer he consumes, Prescott – who in 2010 accepted a peerage after many years of gamely professing his distaste for such honours – is a part of the apparatus of capitalist political control.

Class is not primarily a matter of one's accent, consumption habits, place of birth, or whether one performs manual or mental labour. Put simply, the working class is the source of profit for capitalists. It is the dispossessed class: its members have no capital, no control over the overall conditions of their lives and nothing to live upon but their ability to work for a wage. Workers may possess a house and a car and may even have some 'disposable income'; but they must nevertheless sell their labour power to an employer in return for a liveable wage. Workers' material interests are to obtain better living and working conditions from capitalists, and ultimately – as the only revolutionary class – to destroy capitalism. The objective of the capitalist, however, is to increase exploitation and profits while reducing costs. Since the conflict between these interests is irreconcilable, the principal propaganda role of the capitalist media is, as Marx and Engels succinctly put it in *The German Ideology*, to 'present a particular interest as general or the "general interest" as ruling'. The capitalist media must convince workers that their true interests lie in supporting capitalism (presented as 'the national interest') and that the interests of workers and capitalists are congruous, such that – whether in war, industrial action, economic or environmental crisis – we are 'all in it together'.

2

Not neoliberalism: why the state is still the enemy

State is the name of the coldest of all cold monsters, and coldly it tells lies, and this lie drones on from its mouth: 'I, the State, am the people' – Friedrich Nietzsche, *Thus Spoke Zarathustra*

In the news discourse of contemporary liberal democratic countries, the word 'state' is often damned by association with fascism, Stalinism and other 'authoritarian' political forms. Hence the liberal media's condemnation of today's 'Chinese state media', whose distortions of reality are implicitly counterposed to the supposed openness of democratic media systems. For the British news media, 'our' state is not an organ of oppression, but protective and benevolent – often to a fault. *The Sun* (13 January 2010), for example, expresses its outrage that some Muslims possessed of the temerity to have protested against the British invasion of Afghanistan are 'living on more than £1,000-a-month in State handouts'. One could almost be forgiven for imagining that the state is a kind of charitable fund existing solely for the benefit of undeserving malcontents.

In reality, it is the capitalist class that controls and, through its politicians, directs the state in its own interests. As the eighteenth-century economist Adam Smith made plain in a lecture delivered to his students at the University of Glasgow:

Laws and government may be considered in this and indeed in every case as a combination of the rich to oppress the poor, and preserve to themselves the inequality of the goods which would otherwise be soon destroyed by the attacks of the poor.

Smith's simple observation remains valid today. In a parliamentary system, state power is certainly contested by several political parties; yet each of these factions serves the interests of the national bourgeoisie. Communists reject all of these factions along with the charade of elections, which, as Lenin remarked dryly in *State and Revolution*, serve only 'to decide once every few years, which member of the ruling class is to repress and crush the people through parliament'. One of the key functions of the news and current affairs media, this book argues, is to maintain public faith in the democratic nature of the capitalist dictatorship. Each capitalist faction stakes its claim, on news and current affairs programmes, to be more progressive than its rival. Yet below the frothing surface of parliamentary debate flow the deep currents of capitalist power, which are driven along by a formidable, unelected state apparatus, incorporating the civil service, the police force and the army. The task of the working class, as Marx and Engels proposed, is to overthrow the dictatorship of this state and ultimately to precipitate the classless society known as communism – a society without wage labour or nation states in which workers organise production for their own benefit rather than the profit of capitalists.

Across the globe today, poverty, hunger, warfare, terrorism and environmental chaos reign. Even in the heart of the 'developed' world, workers are experiencing worsening conditions of employment, increasing working hours and shrinking salaries and benefits. For communists, these phenomena are not accidental. Nor are they the consequence of the operations of God or Fate, or of the machinations of rascally or demented world leaders, as implied by liberals' facile jokes about 'evil' and 'stupid' conservative politicians from Ronald Reagan to George W. Bush (one thinks here of Gore Vidal's supercilious attacks on conservative 'dumb-dumbs'). Rather, for communists, the horrors of contemporary capitalism should be explained in material terms as the consequences of the bourgeoisie's desperate quest to extract more profit from the working class and the natural environment under economic conditions – a falling rate of profit and increasing reliance on debt – that increasingly thwart its ambitions.

John Dewey once remarked that 'government is the shadow cast by big business over society'. The state plays a key role in maintaining the domination of the capitalist class. In fact, without a state to regulate and coordinate the system of competition, market competitors would tear one another, and society, to pieces. The nation state thus functions as what Engels, in *Anti-Dühring*, called the 'ideal collective body of all capitalists', regulating the chaos that arises as capitalist interests compete. Liberals, leftists and 'anti-globalisation' activists often complain that the role of the nation state is being usurped by transnational powers such as the International Monetary Fund and the World Bank. Yet as the International Communist Current reminds us in its 2009 article 'The Myth of Globalisation', these organisations 'were set up by American imperialism and have operated in its interest ever since. The World Trade Organisation has a slightly broader base but is still the tool of a small number of capitalist countries'. Indeed, despite the global, deterritorialised nature of the capitalist market, the nation state form remains indispensable for capitalism. In her book *Territory, Authority, Rights*, Saskia Sassen has convincingly argued that the forces of 'globalisation', far from abolishing the nation state, operate within it – just as surely as the nation state exists within the global order. Thus, while elements of the nation state have been 'denationalized', the state retains its vital role in capitalist organisation. 'No other institution', as Ellen Meiksins Wood writes in *Empire of Capital*, 'has even begun to replace the nation state as an administrative and coercive guarantor of social order, property relations, stability of contractual predictability, or any of the other basic conditions required by capital in its everyday life'.

Left-liberals typically translate the critique of capitalism into a concern about neoliberalism, that is, about the transference of certain economic and social responsibilities from the state to the market. Yet while the tag neoliberalism accurately names certain trends towards deregulation and privatisation in particular economic areas since the 1970s, capitalism's very survival over the last century has been premised upon an increasing fusion of state and market. At the end of the nineteenth century, Kautsty observed in *The Class Struggle* that the state was being forced to 'take into its own hands more and more functions'. In 1915, Bukharin noted in 'Toward a theory of the imperialist state' that capitalism had entered a statist phase and Trotsky observed in 1919 that the 'statification of economic life' made it 'impossible to return [...] to free competition'. This analysis was widely endorsed by communist groups and individual revolutionaries in subsequent decades and is borne out by economic data: both in the UK and US, government spending as a proportion of Gross Domestic Product, while largely static throughout the nineteenth century, began to grow massively the 1920s. In our own time, large-scale banking bailouts remind us that states intervene constantly in the operations of the markets in order to maintain the conditions for capital accumulation, while massive standing armies are used to conquer new markets – a situation completely unknown in the nineteenth century. In fact, from the perspective of the *longue durée*, the scope and power of the state can be argued to have increased dramatically since the early twentieth century, when, in the face of the proletarian threat and the difficulties posed by the relative saturation of global markets, the *laissez-faire* capitalism of the nineteenth century gave way to the statified planning regimes of Stalinism, fascism and social democracy. But however that may be, the communist task involves the destruction of the capitalist state *per se*, rather than neoliberalism or some other supposed configuration of it.

The role of the state, in essence, is to create and enforce the laws that facilitate the domination of each national bourgeoisie over its 'own' domestic working class and its rival nation states (to gain a sense of the intensity of these rivalries we need only call to mind the regular demonisation of China in the British and US media today). Each national ruling class takes great pains to prevent any challenge to its dictatorship through sanctions, surveillance, intimidation, torture, terrorism, bombing and genocide conducted by what Louis Althusser forbiddingly termed the Repressive State Apparatuses of the police, army and secret services. But the state – as Gramsci, following Machiavelli, had it – is centaur-like: half beast and half human. Capitalist nation states maintain power not only through naked repression, but through the unceasing propaganda of what Althusser called the Ideological State Apparatuses, such as churches, families, schools, universities and – pre-eminently in today's world – the mass media.

3

Normalising the unthinkable: news media as state propaganda

The class which has the means of material production at its disposal has control at the same time over the means of mental production, so that thereby, generally speaking, the ideas of those who lack the means of mental production are subject to it – Karl Marx and Friedrich Engels, *The German Ideology*

Over the last century, the media have become the key means by which ruling class ideology is disseminated. This does not mean – as critics of Marxism are wont to imply – that communists consider media audiences to be passive dupes, uncritically absorbing all that they see and hear. Such an argument would amount to a counsel of despair. Communists do argue, however, that media audiences, lacking control of the media, are largely subjected to the capitalist media's construction of reality. In his 'Critique of the Situationist International', Gilles Dauvé updates the famous formulation of Marx and Engels:

As capital tends to produce everything as capital, to parcelize everything so as to recompose it with the help of market relations, it also makes of representation a specialized sector of production. Stripped of the means of their material existence, wage-workers are also stripped of the means of producing their ideas, which are produced by a specialized sector [...] The proletarian receives these representations (ideas, images, implicit associations, myths) as he receives from capital the other aspects of his life. Schematically speaking, the nineteenth century worker produced his ideas (even reactionary ones) at the café, the bar or the club, while today's worker sees his on television.

The class warfare of the bourgeoisie against the working class is waged constantly in a maelstrom of media propaganda that seeks to justify capitalism, 'normalising the unthinkable', to borrow Edward Herman's phrase.

The naturalisation of the concept of wage labour over the last two hundred years illustrates the extraordinary efficacy of this process. Wage labour – the capitalist form of work – has come to be accepted as the basis of human life only after centuries of harsh enforcement and patient propaganda work. In an earlier phase of capitalism, the working class press condemned wage labour unequivocally. In the enormously popular radical British newspapers of the nineteenth century, such as Henry Hetherington's *The Poor Man's Guardian*, wage labour was understood as an outrage against humanity whose essential continuity with earlier forms of bondage found expression in the now antiquated phrase 'wage slavery'. Hetherington fulminated against the bourgeoisie in his newspaper, warning them that 'it is the cause of the rabble we advocate, the poor, the suffering, the industrious, the productive classes. We will teach this rabble their power – we will teach them that they are your master, instead of being your slaves'. Despite their popularity, working class newspapers such as *The Poor Man's Guardian* were pushed aside in the nineteenth century by the commercial newspapers, whose attractiveness to advertisers allowed them to meet the increasing costs of newspaper production, despite their smaller circulations. Today, no radical press exists and any challenge to the system of wage labour has become unthinkable in the mass media. Thus, in a period of austerity, the BBC's Sunday morning television discussion programme *The Big Questions* asks 'Is It Time For A Maximum Wage?' (13 March 2010); but it cannot question the legitimacy of the wages system itself. Throughout the mainstream media, exploitation is accepted as a fact of life or *doxa*: in Bourdieu's terms, a powerfully controlling but universally and unconsciously adopted disposition. Once such *doxa* gain general acceptance their parameters can be expanded. Governments across Europe are currently proposing to raise the age of retirement (on the risible pretext of 'protecting' older people's 'right to work') – part of a range of austerity measures being adopted by European states to make the working class pay for the debt crisis. Today, not only is wage labour universally accepted as normal, but the very concept of retirement – a brief period during which older workers are relieved of the burden of wage labour in the final years of their lives – is now threatened with eradication. The media play a key role in normalising such attacks: commenting on French protests against proposals to raise retirement age by two years on BBC1's *Breakfast* programme (16 October 2010), presenter Nicholas Owen expressed his puzzlement that the protesters were concerned by such a trifling extension of their working lives, prompting his interviewee, journalist Bénédicte Paviot, to agree that the public concern did indeed seem 'extraordinary'.

The power of media propaganda to shape our perceptions of the most fundamental aspects of our lives is exercised neither haphazardly nor clumsily. It is a widespread misconception that propaganda involves bludgeoning media audiences with the kinds of lies, crude stereotypes or obvious symbols of state power made familiar by Nazi propaganda films such as *The Eternal Jew* or *Triumph of the Will*. A closely related assumption is that state propaganda necessarily involves the direct dictation of the news agenda by representatives of the state, as tends to happen in statified capitalist countries such as China. But such egregious methods of media control are not especially common in liberal capitalist states. It is true that the British news media do often disseminate lies or fabrications, as we shall see later in this book. It is also true that Western media propaganda can assume a theatrical character: at the time of writing in 2010, British television news regularly broadcasts footage of the military cortèges that frequently process through the English town of Wootton Bassett; as the coffins of dead British soldiers, draped in the national flag, are paraded through the streets, reporters talk solemnly of the soldiers' 'sacrifice' for 'their country'. In a more populist vein, BBC1's live event *Concert for Heroes* (12 September 2010) mixes tributes to the armed services and monarchy with celebrity performances, helping to galvanise support for the British military. Such nationalist spectacles are perhaps the most blatant manifestations of capitalist propaganda today. Mostly, however, liberal capitalist propaganda is more sophisticated than this. Henry Giroux's description of US propaganda as 'more nuance, less theatrical, more cunning, less concerned with repressive modes of control than with manipulative modes of consent' also applies to propaganda in other liberal countries, such as Britain.

The basic mechanisms of news media control are identified in Noam Chomsky and Edward Herman's classic 1988 book *Manufacturing Consent*. Chomsky and Herman outline a 'propaganda model' according to which the output of the news media is 'filtered' in a number of ways so that it comes to reflect dominant political interests. The ownership and 'profit orientation' of media companies, they point out, ensure that the media generally present a view of the world in line with the business interests of their proprietors (as George Orwell wrote in 'Freedom of the Press', 'the British press is extremely centralised, and most of it is owned by wealthy men who have every motive to be dishonest on certain important topics'). The demands of the advertisers who finance the commercial media also place severe restrictions upon what can and cannot be expressed. Chomsky and Herman identify 'flak' as a further filtering mechanism: on those occasions when media workers or institutions step out of line ideologically, representatives of business or the state may be called upon to discipline them. When a report by the BBC Radio 4 journalist Andrew Gilligan raised questions about the validity of the British government's case for the invasion of Iraq in 2003, for example, the government launched a furious attack on the organisation, culminating in the infamous Hutton Report, which savaged the BBC's journalistic standards.

The Hutton furore provides a spectacular example of media control by flak. Yet as Chomsky and Herman suggest, the ideological regulation of the news media is normally achieved discreetly. In a process that has intensified since *Manufacturing Consent* was written, journalists tend to rely on governmental or corporate sources for information and quotations, ensuring that there is little deviation from capitalist agendas. In 2010, to take just one example, the Director General of the supposedly 'independent' BBC met with representatives of the government and the opposition to discuss how best to report the coalition government's savage cuts to public spending (ultimately euphemised by the both the government and the BBC as a 'public spending review'). As the BBC's director of news and current affairs Richard Francis confirmed many years ago in a *New Statesman* article (20 April 1979), BBC journalists covering political stories 'find it natural to ask "an important person" – a senior civil servant or a government minister, for instance – for they are the very people whose decisions largely determine how things will be run in our democracy'. Francis's comment indicates another of Chomsky and Herman's key points, namely, that elite news journalists undergo a lengthy process of accommodation to capitalism, learning during their upbringing and training to absorb the dominant worldview as their own and to ignore alternative viewpoints.

It is sometimes argued by liberals on both sides of the Atlantic (such as Will Hutton in *The World We're In* and Eric Alterman in *What Liberal Media?*) that the news produced by European 'public

23

service' broadcasters is regulated to ensure 'impartiality' and is therefore both less politically conservative and more 'balanced' than that produced by purely commercial news organisations, particularly in countries such as the US. But as the central chapters of this book demonstrate, public service broadcasters reinforce capitalist ideology with impressive consistency, while the significant public trust placed in organisations such as the BBC makes them ideal vehicles for state propaganda. Moreover, journalistic notions of balance and impartiality are extremely narrowly conceived, even within the hallowed precincts of public service broadcasting. In fact, despite the common belief that it strives for impartiality, the BBC is committed to observing only what it calls *'due* impartiality': this means that since the organisation is required to uphold the values of parliamentary democracy, it is *not* required to be impartial towards those – such as communists – who might seek to undermine those values by 'violent, unparliamentary or illegal means' (as the 1977 Annan Report on British broadcasting put it). It is therefore unsurprising that the reporting of political news on British television primarily concentrates upon the positions and policies of the main political parties, as Mike Wayne and Craig Murray have shown in a recent study.

As Philip Schlesinger argued in his classic study of BBC news, *Putting 'Reality' Together*, news reporting can be described as impartial only in relation to the attenuated array of parliamentary opinions. Since they exceed and confound the discursive parameters of parliamentary politics, communist perspectives are unrepresented in the media. A communist critique of the media must therefore draw upon critical frameworks that lie beyond the purview of media punditry and journalistic analysis. The virtual exclusion of working class politics from media agendas also requires the adoption of what Steven Lukes calls a 'three dimensional' view of power that identifies not only the behaviours, conflicts and subjective policy decisions that the media makes visible, but also the hidden agendas, potential issues, latent conflicts and real interests that it elides. By drawing upon the writings of revolutionary groups and individuals as well as academic research, this book attempts to meet these requirements.

4

Blaming the victims, eroding solidarity: two media discourses on immigration

> The history of labor is also the history of competition and discrimination within the working class, dividing the Irish from the British workers, the Algerian from the French, the black from the white, new immigrants from early settlers, and so on, almost universally – Paul Mattick, *Marxism: Last Refuge of the Bourgeoisie?*

Reproaching vulnerable groups for instigating or perpetuating social disorder is a time-honoured journalistic practice. Following the Haitian earthquake of 2010, the BBC's Matt Frei noted in a television news report that 'looting is the only industry', adding that the 'dignity of Haiti's past is long forgotten'. As John Pilger noted (*New Statesman*, 1 February 2010), Frei 'seemed on the point of hyperventilating as he brayed about the "violence" and the "need for security"'. In the aftermath of an earthquake in Chile a few weeks later, BBC television news again concentrated on looters, while the *Channel 4 News* (1 March 2010) reporter Jonathan Rugman noted with weary disdain that 'looters were back at work for a second day, fighting over toilet rolls at a supermarket'. But if the hapless victims of remote disasters are too distant to merit the sympathy of journalists, the most abject individuals in contemporary Western societies – poor immigrants – seldom fare any better.

The working class is a class of migrants. While television commercials celebrate the free-ranging lifestyles of global citizen-consumers, economic insecurity, persecution, and the ravages of imperialist wars force vast numbers of people to migrate from their homes to seek work in other cities or countries, often at enormous physical, psychological and economic risk to themselves and their families. As they scramble to find a place of relative safety from economic or physical violence, so-called 'illegal' immigrants often face blackmail, intimidation, physical and sexual attacks and even death. Each year, many migrants die attempting to enter countries such as the United Kingdom and many prefer to commit suicide rather than be returned to their 'countries of origin', where they often face torture or execution. Even many 'legal' immigrants are super-exploited, working excessively long hours on the lowest rungs of society with little or no job protection.

Across the British media, however, sympathy for the plight of immigrants is in short supply. The Sky1 documentary *UK Border Force* (2008-) follows the UK authorities' hunt for illegal immigrants, or 'clandestines', to use the official newspeak adopted by the documentary's narrator (compare 'asylum seekers' – another nominalisation whose bureaucratic tone fails to mitigate its connotations of illegitimacy). As a voiceover at the start of each programme sternly explains, the authorities featured in the documentary are seeking the 'law-breakers and impostors who don't have a right to be here'. Describing the first series of the programme, Sky's web site further elucidates the premise of the programme: 'for the first time, the cameras show exactly how our UK borders are protected and how immigrants and visitors to Britain are dealt with on the front line'. The web site's description of the British state's borders as 'ours', together with the military connotations of 'protection' and 'the front line', imply that the state is engaged in heroic struggle against cunning foreign invaders, rather than the harassment and repression of some of society's most desperate individuals.

In episode 2 of the documentary's first series, a woman from Moldova who has been working illegally at a hotel on the Isle of Wight is returned to her country of origin, despite her claims that she had been abused there. As she breaks down in tears, an officer regretfully remarks to the camera that despite being a 'sweet lady' she is 'still an offender, just like everybody else'. In episode 8 of the same series, officials in Calais search lorries for illegal immigrants, eventually discovering a group of petrified Indians hiding among the cargo in the back of a lorry at Dover; as the immigrants blink in the torchlight, an officer remarks nonchalantly that Indians tend to be among 'the most compliant' stowaways. In the final episode of the programme's second series, *UK Border Force 2*, an elderly Chinese lady is discovered working illegally as a child-minder at a restaurant in Wales, having apparently having paid a gang master to smuggle her into the UK. The terrified lady is arrested for illegal entry and removed from the restaurant premises. Although *UK Border Force* affords its audience some very brief glimpses into the miserable living and working conditions endured by many illegal immigrants, the programme's framing and mode of address privilege the perspective of the immigration officials and serve to minimise the viewer's sympathy for the immigrants. Indeed, overall, *UK Border Force* illustrates the distinctive mode of media propaganda in liberal democratic societies: social 'issues' such as immigration are not entirely ignored, but are seen through the lens of ruling class ideology, frustrating attempts to comprehend them in relation to the totality of capitalist social relations.

Immigrants of all kinds are routinely demonised as scroungers or criminals in political and media discourse. The Labour Party, for example, explicitly links immigrants with delinquency in a section in its 2010 election manifesto entitled 'Crime and Immigration', while elements of the British news media – particularly the right-wing press – regularly bemoan the 'cost to the taxpayer' of the benefit payments made to immigrants. Thus a *Daily Express* (13 December 2006) headline complains about Britain's £110 million annual 'bill' for local authority translation services aimed at what the newspaper calls the number of homeless Eastern European immigrants in and around the city. Officers from Peterborough City Council, Cambridgeshire Constabulary and the UKBA threatened rough-sleeping immigrants who had not worked for the past three months with removal to 'their own country', as Labour's Border and Immigration Minister Phil Woolas phrased it. Media reports of the repatriation scheme were less than sympathetic towards those affected. A *Daily Express* article (7 April 2010), for example, noted that in the woodland in which some of the Peterborough immigrants were living, 'clothes lines were slung between the trees and an empty cider bottle lay outside one tent' – the latter detail suggesting that the immigrants were not only trespassers, but anti-social alcoholics.

The liberal media matched the right-wing press in expressions of callousness towards the migrants' situation. A *Channel 4 News* (7 April 2010) feature about the pilot scheme began with a brief interview with a Russian man who had lost his agricultural job. Now sleeping in a tent, the man faced deportation. The interview was followed by short extracts from interviews with Labour's Phil Woolas and representatives of the other political parties, who, rather than expressing sympathy for the immigrants, strove to outdo one another in condemnation of them. A Conservative politician claimed that the Peterborough scheme was 'too little and too late' and that Labour had been wrong 'not to have moratorium on free movement'. A Liberal Democrat politician, meanwhile, claimed that the 'problem' had been caused by the government's underestimation of the numbers of immigrants, adding that 'now we are suffering the consequences'. The news report ended with a brief extract of an interview with a local *Big Issue* vendor, who, having experienced homelessness himself, might have been expected to harbour some sympathy for the immigrants. If anything, however, the vendor's final words in the interview extract – 'a lot of people feel they're jumping in and taking their position' – echoed the politicians' view of the immigrants as unruly interlopers.

Clearly, much media discourse about immigration issues, even in the liberal media, is aimed at discouraging solidarity with immigrant populations. In his article 'Getting to the Roots of Radical Politics Today', Bauman points to the metonymic function of anti-immigrant discourse and to the potential for its political manipulation:

> Chasing the migrants away, one rebels (by proxy) against all those mysterious global forces that threaten to visit on everybody else the fate already suffered by the migrants. There is a lot of capital in that illusion that can be (and is) adroitly exploited by the politicians.

Controversies over immigration, then, have a huge potential to divide the working class. Media attacks on immigrant scapegoats encourage non-immigrant workers in the belief that they are privileged – that they can somehow be exempted from the social and economic insecurity that increasingly engulfs the working class as a whole.

The divisiveness of much media coverage of immigration may be illustrated by a brief analysis of a BBC *Panorama* documentary entitled 'Is Britain Full?' (19 April 2010), which was broadcast just weeks before a British general election in which immigration policy was a key 'doorstep issue'. The question form of the film's title implies a certain disinterestedness. Yet the title also presupposes a nationalist perspective, posing the question of 'immigration control' from the point of view of the British state, which, at the time of the broadcast, was becoming increasingly protectionist in response to an entrenched economic crisis. The programme's investigative reporter, John Ware, focused on the economic requirements of British businesses. Casting a sceptical eye on the mostly immigrant workforce of the food retail chain Prêt à Manger, Ware questioned whether 'Britain really gains' from high levels of immigration, arguing that immigrants' 'contribution' to the economy is often less than is widely assumed.

'Is Britain Full?' also presented immigration as a threat to the adequate provision of healthcare, housing and education in Britain. At the beginning of the film, Ware visited the maternity ward of a Manchester hospital, asking the mother of a newborn baby boy: 'Do you think about what his quality of life will be?' Later in the film, Ware noted that British schools are 'feeling the pinch' from over-population and asserted that 'migrants *do* lengthen the queue' for housing. By making 'migrants' the subject of his clause and emphasising the causative auxiliary verb, Ware implied that migrants are collectively responsible for the housing shortage. In fact, the imputation of agency to immigrants for actions and policies over which they have little or no control is a widely used technique in the reporting of immigration issues: as a presenter on BBC television's *London News* (17 March 2010) jauntily asked: 'Next: do immigrants really jump ahead of British people on housing waiting lists?'

The anti-immigration thesis of 'Is Britain Full?' is vulnerable to several objections. Despite agreeing with the presenter's premise that Britain could not 'cope' if its population rose to 70 million, Labour's Phil Woolas expressed doubts that this prediction would be borne out and correctly noted that net immigration into the UK was actually falling. It might be added that many areas of Britain are sparsely populated. It is therefore preposterous to attribute the problems experienced by Britons in accessing housing, education and healthcare to the single factor of immigration – or even to immigration at all, since, as Philippe Legrain's book *Your Country Needs Them* establishes, immigrants tend to 'contribute' more to the economy than natives. Rather, the social problems identified in 'Is Britain Full?' are the result of capitalism's systematic misuse of productive resources. Like the larger and graver crises of global starvation and ecological

33

destruction, the problems of inadequate housing, healthcare and education in Britain stem not from over-population, but from the priorities of a political system dedicated to exploitation, profit-making and the pursuit of imperialist war rather than meeting social needs.

'Is Britain Full?' was punctuated by interviews with British politicians, several of whom talked of the need to reduce immigration and to encourage 'economically inactive' Britons into work. This agenda was taken up in the following week's *Panorama* (26 April 2010), which followed the fortunes of four young unemployed men in Swindon. *Panorama*'s presenter Jeremy Vine began by questioning whether such men 'really want to work'. Adopting the conventions of a makeover television programme, the *Panorama* team then brought in the 'heavy artillery' in the form of the businessman Lord Digby Jones in an attempt to 'fire up' the idlers. Jones critiqued the young men's job-seeking efforts, advising two of them to cut their hair in order to set a 'good example'. Jones also advocated the introduction of a US-style workfare system (that is, making receipt of benefits dependent on claimants undertaking training or low-paid and sometimes unpaid work). Crucially, moreover, the programme's various admonitions of the indolent Swindonians were counterbalanced by fulsome praise for the exemplary work ethic of Britain's Polish immigrants.

It is here that we must take a step 'beyond the left' by recognising that pro-immigration discourses can be just as divisive as anti-immigration or racist ones. Following the announcement in 2010 of Conservative plans to impose a cap on overseas immigration, Philippe Legrain, writing in *New Statesman* (27 September 2010), argued that migrants should be welcomed into Britain, not in their own right, but because they 'contribute' disproportionately to the economy and often undertake menial work that British people are not 'prepared' to do – a phrase which implies that British workers tend to reject low-paid or uncongenial work out of indolence. While ostensibly sympathetic towards immigrants, Legrain's argument here is hardly less troubling than the anti-immigrant discourse of the political right, since it endorses the exploitation of immigrants while transferring the stigma of laziness onto the British working class. In a similar vein, the entrepreneur Luke Johnson, writing in *The Financial Times* (3 November 2010), describes immigrants as 'human capital' who are 'vital to our economy' and notes – so patronisingly as to invite admiration – that the 'challenge is not immigration' but 'to educate more natives to take control of their destinies'. Johnson's celebration of immigrants as economic godsends and his chastisement of feckless natives are every bit as corrosive of working class solidarity as the anti-immigrant diatribes of right-wing xenophobes.

Faced with a choice between treating immigrants as scapegoats for the ills of capitalist society and welcoming their potential for disciplining the native 'reserve army of labour' or reducing the capitalists' wage bill, the communist – indeed, the human – response must be to reject both of these discourses. In their place, we should reaffirm Marx's maxim that workers have no country, while struggling towards the creation of a post-capitalist world without wage labour and national borders. The weight of nationalist ideology on working class consciousness is such that radical political transformations of this kind may seem virtually impossible; but to borrow a remark from Marcuse's *One Dimensional Man*, 'the unrealistic sound of these propositions is indicative, not of their utopian character, but of the strength of the forces which prevent their realisation'.

5

Rioters, racists and wreckers: media images of strikers

Events like the Russian Revolution, a great strike, the operation of a nationalized industry, are distorted so as to produce an unfavourable impression of their nature upon the citizen who learns of their character from his newspaper – Harold Laski, *Politics*

The exploitation of workers is the very lifeblood of capitalism. It follows that strikes – organised withdrawals of labour power – are the pre-eminent weapon of the working class against its employers. By striking, workers rebel against exploitation and the alienation that wage labour engenders. It is therefore unsurprising that the capitalist news media have always tended to undermine strikers and their struggles. In its very earliest days, the BBC proved its worth as a vehicle of state propaganda during the 1926 General Strike by banning the voices of strikers and supporting the state in the name of the 'national interest' – all the while maintaining a veneer of impartiality. As the BBC's first Director General John Reith wrote frankly of the government in his diaries: 'they want to be able to say that they did not commandeer us, but they know that they can trust us not to be really impartial'. In fact, despite perennial concerns that the BBC's Reithian heritage is being eroded or neglected, Reith's support for the British state in the face of industrial action has proved to be an enduring legacy. The Glasgow University Media Group's study *Really Bad News* shows that both BBC and ITN television news reports about the British Leyland dispute in 1972, for example, consistently privileged the arguments of employers and the state over those of the strikers.

Perhaps the most notorious example of political bias in the reporting of strikes remains the BBC's *Nine O'Clock News* coverage of the police charge on miners during a picket of Orgreave coking plant in south Yorkshire in 1984. What became known as the 'Battle of Orgreave' was a pivotal event not only in the 1984-85 Miners' Strike, but in the recent history of British industrial relations. On 13 June 1984, riot police, some mounted on horses, attacked unarmed strikers. By the time the BBC's footage was shown on the news five days later, however, it had been edited to show the miners advancing first and the police seeming to respond in self-defence. At the 'Orgreave riot trial' in Sheffield Crown Court in 1985, 50 participants in the Orgreave demonstration were charged with riot, conspiracy and other offences. But the strikers' defence lawyers raised questions about the BBC's footage, arguing that public opinion had been unfairly influenced by the editors of the *Nine O'Clock News*. The prosecution case collapsed; yet to this date, no details of any BBC investigation into the incident have been made public.

The emphasis on the strikers' violence in the BBC's Orgreave footage was consistent with the wider media framing of the strike. Reporters concentrated on 'picket line violence', a phrase that worked by association to cast the pickets, rather than the police, as the instigators of the violence. Miners themselves criticised television news content for its anti-striker bias and actively tried to shift the news agenda towards the closure of so-called 'uneconomic pits'. Yet the media's framing of the dispute was heavily influenced by powerful interests. According to Greg Philo ('Audience beliefs and the 1984/5 miners' strike'), a diary of the strike kept by journalist Michael Crick recorded that news desks were supplied daily with National Coal Board reports about the numbers of strikers returning to work as the strike came to an end. Although the validity of the NCB figures was challenged by some journalists and the National Union of

Mineworkers, the figures were mostly accepted by journalists. As Crick wrote in his strike diary, journalists also 'generally adopted the board's phrase "the drift back to work" despite its suggestion of a continuous and inevitable process'. A quarter of a century later, the news reporting of the Miners' Strike remains an exemplary instance of media bias through the manipulation of words and images.

Yet the reporting of some more recent industrial disputes gives some new twists to the hegemonic media discourse on strikes and strikers. On 28 January 2009, contract workers began a wildcat strike at the Total oil refinery in Lindsey, eastern England, the third largest oil refinery in the UK. The dispute centred on plans to reduce the number of local contractors working on an expansion project at the refinery, as workers from Italy and Portugal were given work contracts (the UK's general trade union, the GMB, subsequently claimed to have irrefutable proof that these workers were paid less than local workers). While there was no threat to existing employment, workers feared that jobs could be lost when a 'no sacking' agreement between unions and Total bosses ended the following month. Between 800 and 1,000 workers gathered at the refinery and immediately voted for a strike. Insisting that workers follow normal procedure for industrial conflicts, the Unite union's shop stewards' committee resigned *en masse* in order to distance the union from the illegal strike. Yet the industrial action recurred throughout 2009. In June, for example, Total claimed that 1,200 contractors had walked out on unofficial strike over planned redundancies and that 600 workers were protesting outside the refinery.

In the British media, the Total strike was initially framed not as a defence of the collective agreement, but as a defence of 'British jobs' against the incursions of 'foreign workers'. This nationalist perspective was not entirely a media fabrication. In the strike's early days, some pickets and demonstrators certainly did sport placards, some of them bearing the logo of the Unite union and the slogan of the Prime Minister, Gordon Brown: 'British jobs for British workers'. The construction workers' web site BearFacts, which was a highly influential information source during the strike, also promoted the 'British jobs for British workers' slogan – even though this was not a strike demand – and some comments made on the BearFacts discussion forums were stridently nationalistic in tone.

But this does not tell the whole story. Beyond the 'grassroots' expressions of nationalism, the news media also formatted the strike as an outburst of chauvinism, as though the presence of 'foreign workers' were the strikers' primary concern. Seeking to exploit the strike for its own ends, the newspaper of the neo-fascist National Front, *Nationalist News*, predictably reproduced the 'British Jobs for British Workers' motto as a headline. The mainstream press and television news media – ordinarily quiet when workers engage in unofficial action or illegal solidarity strikes – also devoted considerable coverage to the Lindsey struggle, mostly adopting a nationalist perspective on events. Philip Johnson, in *The Daily Telegraph* (31 January 2009), lamented 'the wave of stoppages at oil refineries in protest at the employment of foreign workers', chastising the Labour Party for failing to deliver on its promises of employment for British workers. Iain Macwhirter of *The Herald* (2 February 2009) also characterised the strike as xenophobic, contrasting the unseem-liness of the Lindsey strikers with the integrity of those taking part in populist demonstrations against banking bailouts in France. BBC and ITV news, too, framed the strike as a protest against 'foreign workers'. The BBC's editing of an interview with a Lindsey striker even generated an Orgreave-style controversy. In a sound bite broadcast on the *BBC News at Ten* (2 February 2009), the worker makes a comment that seems to express nation-alist bigotry: 'these Portuguese and Eye-ties', he remarks, 'we can't work alongside of them'. Yet on the more exhaustive news discussion programme *Newsnight*, broadcast on BBC2 later the same evening, a slightly longer version of the same interview extract was broadcast: 'These Portuguese and Eye-ties, we can't work alongside of them; they're segregated'. Through its inclusion of the additional, explanatory clause, the second interview clip creates quite a different impression to the first, suggesting a desire for solidarity with the 'foreign' workers – from whom the British workers were forcibly segregated by their employers – rather than aversion towards them.

By the time the BBC issued a public apology for its *News at Ten* 'mistake', the propaganda potential of the broadcast had already been realised (one might add here that such admissions of 'mistakes' tend to humanise those in power, clearing the way for further abuses; hence the routine description by contemporary Labour politicians of the Iraq war as a mistake). Mistake or not, the *News at Ten* report was consistent with the media's general framing of the strike as an expression of British workers' resentment of, and antipathy towards, their European counterparts: one BBC television news reporter even talked of 'foreign workers' living in an off-shore 'hotel' (in fact, an ex-prison ship), giving the impression of a privileged foreign workforce. A few days into the strike, however, the nationalist slogans were being diffused and some strikers even brandished banners calling for overseas workers to join the strikes. Indeed, in defiance of the attempts to divide the workforce along national lines, workers from overseas joined wildcat strikes at refineries, building sites and power stations all over the UK. In early February 2009, for example, 600 power station workers, including many Polish workers, went on a wildcat strike at the Langage power station near Plymouth. Consequently, when Total sacked 640 Lindsey workers in June 2009, the media was much less able to frame the ensuing wave of solidarity strikes as xenophobic. Largely divested of nationalistic overtones, the summer strikes attracted less media attention than the winter ones, yet they were

41

successful for the workers, forcing Total to reinstate the 640 sacked Lindsey workers. The outcome of the strikes demonstrated the power of working class solidarity to overcome the nationalist divisions fostered by the employers, the unions and the media. As Martin Glaberman emphasises in *Working for Wages*, it is absurd to expect the working class to be perfect before it makes the revolution, since – as the workers at Lindsey showed – it is only through collective struggle that the suffocating weight of bourgeois ideology can begin to be lifted.

It could be argued that the British media's coverage of the Lindsey strikes created and exploited a notion of the Lindsey workers as 'bad nationalists'. A double standard is at work here: it is, after all, the ruling class, with its immigration laws and imperialist wars (and in the specific case of Lindsey management, its segregation of workers by national origin) whose outlook is fundamentally nationalist. Indeed, media attacks on working class xenophobia serve not only to fracture working class solidarity but also to conceal the nationalist perspective of each ruling class, as it seeks to subdue its 'own' workers and outcompete its international rivals. This 'good' nationalism contrasts with the 'bad' nationalism of the Lindsey workers, who were constructed as backward chauvinists – the *wrong kind* of patriots.

In this respect, the news media's construction of the Lindsey workers deviates somewhat from its typical presentation of strikers. As the Glasgow Media Group's study of the news coverage of the 1972 Leyland strike suggests, the media normally casts strikers as unpatriotic wreckers of the national interest. Indeed, it remains the case that the media tends to accuse strikers of 'holding the country to ransom', as the clichéd tabloid phrase has it. When strikes take place in public-facing industries, for example, the media can usually be relied upon to emphasize the public inconvenience they cause. The *Daily Mirror* (22 October 2009) began a leader article on the 2009 postal strike at Royal

Mail, for example, with the comment that:

> There are no winners – only losers – in the Royal Mail strikes. The public may not get letters and parcels they're looking forward to. Businesses will lose cash when they're unable to fulfil offers. Bosses will fail to deliver the service they are paid handsomely to provide. Striking postal workers will be out of pocket when a day or two of wages are docked.

Notably, the *Mirror*'s leader contains no discussion of the workers' demands, or their reasons for striking; instead, their action is couched in instrumentalist terms as an inconvenience that must be quickly 'sorted out'. Moreover, by presenting a strike as a situation in which everybody loses and the avoidance of a strike as a win-win scenario, the article implies that the interests of bosses and workers are ultimately reconcilable – that they are 'in it together'.

The long-running British Airways cabin crew strikes, undertaken in response to the company's plans to reduce the number of its cabin crew and withdraw their 'perks', has attracted similar media coverage. Some newspapers have starkly advised BA workers to support their bosses or face unemployment: 'BA crew must realise it's either survival of the fittest or extinction', warned Alasdair Osborne in *The Daily Telegraph* (31 July 2010). But appeals to a notion of the broader 'public good' have also been widespread and the potential for 'passenger disruption' has dominated stories about the BA strike. The *Daily Mail* (20 February 2010) opened a report with the comment that 'thousands of families could have their Easter holiday plans ruined as British Airways cabin crew prepare to strike', while a front page *Guardian* article about Unite's postponement of a BA strike ballot (28 June 2010) began with the observation that 'the prospect of a summer of discontent for British Airways passengers receded yesterday' and a *Times* lead article (19 May

2010) advised the BA workforce 'to stop thinking only of themselves, and start thinking of their company, the economy, and most of all, their passengers'. As the communist group International Communist Tendency writes in its online article 'Class War at BA':

> Predictably enough, the media have almost universally lined up against the strikers, concentrating coverage for the most part on the inconvenience to the travelling public, breaking off now and then to point out how well paid BA workers are in comparison with other sectors of the industry in a period when BA are making losses.

Framing strikes as public inconveniences clearly helps to erode public support for the cause of strikers, whose opinions are seldom registered in news reports.

For all factions of the ruling class and the media to express open hostility towards workers' struggles would, however, be foolhardy. Both capitalists and the left-wing media recognise the important role played by the unions in mediating industrial disputes. Here the coverage of the BA cabin crew dispute is again instructive. Initially, the Unite union's ballot for strike action in May 2010 had been declared illegal on a technicality, causing Seumas Milne, in *The Guardian* (20 May 2010), to worry that 'the right to strike in Britain is now under serious threat'. Unite ultimately won this right, however, through the Court of Appeal. In an article entitled 'British Airways ruling: When judges came to the aid of the workers', *Guardian* journalist Anne Perkins (21 May 2010) expressed her surprise that the Lord Chief Justice should have allowed the strike to proceed officially. From a communist perspective, however, the move was less than extraordinary. The British ruling class is anything but stupid. Following the wildcat actions at Lindsey in 2009, the bourgeoisie certainly had reason to fear widespread unofficial action by workers: the conservative Policy Exchange think-tank even issued a warning that Britain could be entering a new 'age of militancy' akin to that of the 1970s. The legal endorsement of British Airways staff's 'right to strike' allowed the strike to be controlled by the union, which it quickly did: Unite dropped its opposition to staffing cuts and restricted its demands to the reinstatement of travel 'perks' stripped from striking BA workers. It also took care to isolate the cabin crew strike from the simultaneous dispute at the British airport operator BAA, vastly reducing its efficacy. Indeed, over the past century, the unions – in their support for both imperialist world wars and their role in separating struggling workers by industrial sector, job role or union membership – have tended to serve the interests of capitalism rather than those of workers, however militant their rank and file members may be. By supporting the unions, *The Guardian* and the left-wing press, like the unions themselves, can pose as radical, while implicitly endorsing the legal containment and neutralisation of workers' struggles.

In fact, the advantages of mediating strikes through union and media apparatuses, rather than simply ignoring them, are becoming clear even in those countries whose news media have historically tended to 'black out' news of industrial action. In statified capitalist countries such as China, industrial action often goes unreported. An article in *The Observer* (4 July 2010) noted that reporters covering the massive strike by Honda workers in Guangdong province in May 2010 had 'been ordered to play down their coverage of the strikes to minimise the risk of copycat actions'. In fact, the Chinese Communist Party issued a ban on the reporting of industrial action in Guangdong on 28 May 2010. Nevertheless, in the face of massive workplace struggles, the Chinese ruling class is increasingly turning to liberal democratic methods of legal mediation and media reporting as methods of social control. Workers in Guangdong, for example, are to be granted a legal 'right to strike' for a trial period, while the Chinese media sometimes cover strikes involving foreign-owned companies. This provides valuable propaganda against companies owned by Japanese or South Korean regional rivals and allows strikes to be reported in ways that do not threaten the state. For example, the Chinese media's reporting of the Honda strikes did not mention widespread complaints that thugs linked to the All China Federation of Trade Unions – China's only legally recognized labour organization – were attacking strikers.

As the example of China suggests, there is currently a growing wave of working class resistance to capitalism in every continent. While the news media will be increasingly unable to ignore this unrest, they will certainly seek to manipulate its public representation. The right-wing media will undoubtedly continue to derogate strikers as opponents of the 'national interest' and the 'public good', while the liberal media excoriate strikers as racists or reactionaries (as they did during the Lindsey strike) and reinforce illusions in the progressive potential of the unions. And while occasionally mentioning the immediate *economic* demands of strikers, the capitalist media will most likely continue to ignore the *political* character of strikes as expressions of class revolt against the entire system of exploitation.

6

Greenwashing capitalism: news media and the environment

Oh Perfect Masters / They thrive on disasters – Brian Eno, 'Dead Finks Don't Talk'

The crisis facing what has become known as 'the environment' is one of the most prominent subjects on the global news agenda today. And rightly so. Amongst many other disturbing trends, the 2009 Climate Change Conference in Copenhagen drew attention to recent dramatic changes in 'global mean surface temperature, sea-level rise, ocean and ice sheet dynamics, ocean acidification, and extreme climatic events', adding that 'there is a significant risk that many of the trends will accelerate, leading to an increasing risk of abrupt or irreversible climactic shifts'. Indeed, while scientists may disagree about the timescales involved, there is no serious doubt that the global environment is facing a crisis that will massively impact upon its ability to support human life unless it is urgently addressed. There is also little scientific doubt that this crisis is largely the result of human activity (and even where this is not so – as in the case of the planet's natural emissions of the greenhouse gas methane – human action is nonetheless required to prevent further environmental damage).

News and current affairs media have not always embraced these arguments. The theory of man-made global warming, for example, has been fiercely disputed in a number of television documentaries. The BBC2 series *Scare Stories* (1997) accused global warming campaigners of being 'driven by passionate belief rather than verifiable fact'. In the same year, Martin

Durkin's Channel 4 documentary *Against Nature* compared environmentalists to Nazis and described them as enemies of science – even if the broadcast was later found by the Independent Television Commission to have misrepresented the views of its interviewees. Ten years later, Channel 4 broadcast another Durkin documentary, *The Great Global Warming Swindle* (2007), which again attempted to discredit the theory of anthropogenic climate change. The programme's arguments and methods were vigorously contested by several scientists, some of whose complaints were upheld by the media regulator Ofcom. The power of the media to misinform the public about environmental issues should not, therefore, be underestimated. Nevertheless, despite the continued opposition to environmentalism by many vested capitalist interests, explicitly envirosceptic arguments are increasingly rare in the contemporary media and, as the reaction to Durkin's documentaries shows, do not go unchallenged by scientists. As the scientific consensus about global warming and other environmental threats has consolidated, the bourgeoisie has mostly come to recognise the material and ideological advantages of making the public pay for the cost of environmental destruction and of exploiting the public's growing environmental awareness through the promotion of 'green' goods and services. In the media, this new consensus is reflected across the ideological spectrum: even the conservative *Daily Express* (13 May 2006), for example, details '50 Ways to Go Green'. Generally speaking, then, contemporary journalism does not reject scientific evidence about global warming or pollution; rather, it assigns the responsibility for solving these problems to the state and, in particular, to the lifestyle choices of individual consumers.

In the summer of 2010, CNN's environmental series *Going Green* broadcast a horrifying report on the Bangladeshi ship breaking yard at Chittagong. The report noted that unsafe practices at the yard are contaminating the soil and polluting fish stocks, while the workers who carve up the freighters and tankers for scrap metal inhale asbestos and suffer appalling injuries owing to a lack of basic health and safety provision. But while the report served as a powerful reminder of the human and environmental impact of capitalism, particularly among poor and working class people, it failed to set the environmental chaos being wrought in such settings within the wider context of the global capitalist economy. It did not mention, for example, the complicity of Western states in the EU and US in outsourcing dangerous and polluting work to poor countries with laxer safety regulations and did not propose a structural solution to the problems it highlighted; to have done so would have undermined *Going Green*'s avowed remit to showcase 'how businesses are balancing their environmental responsibilities with the need for profit' and to profile entrepreneurs 'who fight on the side of Mother Nature'. Like almost all media coverage of environmental issues, *Going Green* can conceive of environmental 'solutions' only within the framework of the profit system.

The pitiful example of Chittagong reminds us that capitalism's degradation of the environment is inextricably bound up with its exploitation of humanity. Class struggle and serious ecological action are thus inseparable – a perspective typically obscured by liberal environmentalists. In his essay 'Victim of Success: Green Politics Today', Paul Kingsnorth endorses Jonathan Porritt's view that both capitalism *and* communism espouse a productivist paradigm in which 'increasing centralisation and large-scale bureaucratic control' contribute to a view of the planet as 'there to be conquered'. This view of communism is shared by many environmentalist writers; yet it relies upon a conflation of communism with Soviet-style state planning that is quite misleading. The Stalinist Soviet Union, with its social classes and wage labour, surely represented a statified form of capitalism rather than communism. Far from regarding nature as a resource that must be subordinated to

49

and encourage us to replace 'uncool' consumer goods, such as mobile telephones, before the end of their useful life ('ashamed of your mobile?', asks one British television advertisement). Maintaining the production cycle in the interests of profit rather than human need thus comes at a huge environmental cost. It might be added here that capitalism also generates a plethora of socially useless, but environmentally damaging jobs in fields ranging from banking to military 'defence', which would be dissolved in a communist society.

The corporations responsible for damaging the environment have every interest in avoiding the costs involved in preventing accidents and minimising pollution. Installing equipment that might prevent or limit environmental damage incurs costs ('externalities') that capitalists naturally prefer to shift onto consumers in the form of pollution. This was horrifically illustrated by the explosion at BP's Deepwater Horizon oil drilling rig in the Gulf of Mexico in 2010, which left 11 men presumed dead and resulted in a huge spillage of crude oil that damaged the ecology of the Gulf Coast. BP had a track record of such 'accidents'. An explosion at a Texas City refinery in 2005 killed 15 workers and injured 170 others; investigators later determined that a warning system had been disabled. A congressional committee report on a leak discovered in BP's pipeline at Prudhoe Bay in Alaska in 2006 also blamed the company's cost-saving shortcuts. Yet BP was not solely to blame either for these disasters or for the Deepwater tragedy. Although US media reports about Deepwater were quick to emphasise that BP is a British company, the US government bore considerable responsibility for the disaster: in 2009, for example, the US government had exempted BP from an environmental review mandated by the National Environmental Policy Act.

Sometimes the state plays an even more direct role in ecological destruction. The manufacture and testing of weapons needed by capitalist states in pursuit of their imperialist ambitions are hugely destructive of the environment – as is warfare itself. Michael Parenti notes in his book *To Kill a Nation: The Attack on Yugoslavia* that the depleted uranium shells used by NATO in the 1990s Balkan wars have caused widespread contamination and human illness over many years: the bombing of a fertilizer factory and a petrochemical plant in just one Serbian city, Pančevo, released into the atmosphere huge quantities of chemicals dangerous to human beings and contaminated the drinking water of ten million people. In the Middle East, to take another example, the inhabitants of the Gaza strip and West Bank – who are among the most defeated working class people in the world – are forced to wash, cook with and sometimes drink untreated water. They are further subjected to regular bombardments by the Israeli army, which tests its drones and other weapons on the area, contaminating the land with phosphorous and heavy metals, which leads to cancers, deformities and other health problems. Similar phenomena have been observed following the allied invasion of Iraq in 2003; for example, child mortality and cancer rates have skyrocketed in Fallujah since the US attacks on the town.

As these examples suggest, it is not the working class, but the ruling class, through its pursuit of profit and imperial dominance, that destroys the environment, together with its human inhabitants. For communists, there can be no serious attempt to address the environmental crisis without the abolition of capitalism and the creation of a society in which production and consumption are collectively organised for human need rather than private profit. Predictably, however, the capitalist media strive to deny this conclusion and to shift the responsibility for capitalism's devastation of the environment onto workers. News and current affairs media tend to generalise the problem of the environment as the responsibility of 'ordinary people' through appeals to become more 'environmentally conscious' or to 'do one's bit' for the environment by recycling and making 'ethical' consumer choices. The public is upbraided for using plastic shopping bags, for buying 'environmentally unfriendly' light bulbs or for excessive air travel. To borrow Judith Butler's phrase, there is a sustained campaign to 'responsibilize' the public for global warming and environmental pollution. The gap between the actions and the public pronouncements of the US politician Al Gore indicates something of the hypocrisy of this crusade. Gore asks the audience of his environmental film-lecture *An Inconvenient Truth* (2006): 'are you ready to change the way you live?'. Yet the Clinton/Gore administration failed to ratify the Kyoto treaty on greenhouse gas emissions or to take any serious action on climate change in the 1990s.

The recent 'ban the bag' campaign in Britain illustrates some of the limitations of green initiatives. In 2007, Rebecca Hosking became a minor celebrity in Britain after launching a campaign to ban plastic shopping bags. The campaign inspired admiring articles about Hosking and prompted eco-campaigns in the British press. For £1.25, the *Daily Mail* (27 February 2008), for example, offered readers an Eco Bag, bearing the sanctimonious legend 'Bags of Ethics'. Yet the environmental impact of the bag ban is questionable. As Rob Lyons has pointed out in *spiked* magazine, plastic carrier bags, as well as being conveniently re-usable in themselves, are produced using a part of crude oil – naphtha – that if not used to produce bags, would mostly be burned off into the atmosphere. While its impact on the environment seems infinitesimal, the bag ban has greatly boosted both the 'green' credentials of the politicians who have supported it and the profits of supermarkets, which can now charge their customers for plastic bags or reusable 'eco bags'.

The sense of personal responsibility for climate change inculcated by such green initiatives also helps to engineer consent for a reduction in living standards. Not only are workers exhorted to undertake unpaid environmentalist labour – such as sorting and driving their household waste to a recycling centre – but they are asked to reduce their consumption. Writing in *The Sun* (12 June 2010), Robert Winston endorses Prince Charles' view that people should 'consume less' in order to save the planet. In similar mode, Jeremy Leggett writes in *The Guardian* (23 January 2010) that we need 'to consume less "stuff" and to seek a type of prosperity outside the conventional trappings of affluence'. As well as ignoring the reality that the average worker earns less in real terms than he or she did three decades ago, such moralistic attacks on working class consumption are highly congenial to ruling class interests, since they bypass the more fundamental question of capitalist production and prepare the working class for austerity.

That workers tend to suffer disproportionately from the implementation of green taxes and other environmental levies is often overlooked in environmentalist discourse. This is nowhere more obvious than in concerns over the availability of 'cheap flights'. Writing in the *Daily Express* (13 May 2006), Penny Poyzer advises flyers to calculate the CO2 cost of their trips and 'to invest an equal amount in renewable energies', while George Marshall in *The Guardian* (13 September 2007) rightly criticises the tokenism of the plastic bag ban and other green strategies and observes that flying causes far greater environmental damage. Marshall is, of course, quite right; but it is also necessary to consider *who* flies and *how often*. Most of those who pay for cheap flights are working class people who fly infrequently and who are in no position to 'invest in renewable energies'. The most frequent flyers, meanwhile, are typically well-paid business-people and politicians, who often buy their 'right to pollute' through carbon offset schemes and the cost of whose flights is usually defrayed by expense accounts. Raising the cost of air travel therefore punishes most heavily those who contribute the least to environmental damage through flying.

News and current affairs media thus help to condition the

working class to accept responsibility for – and absorb the costs of – environmental damage, allowing capitalists to profit from the sale of prestigious and often expensive 'environmentally friendly' products. At the same time, the discourse of 'ethical consumption' tends to reduce action over environmental issues to a series of personal lifestyle choices. As Jodi Dean notes in her book *Democracy and Other Neoliberal Fantasies*, framing the solution to environmental problems as questions of consumer choice only serves to reproduce capitalist ideology:

How would climate change, for example, be rendered into the terms of political identity? Is it a matter of lifestyle? Of being the sort of person who drives a Prius and carries an attractive nylon bag to the grocery store? Such a reduction to an imagined 'green identity' formats climate change as an issue of individual consumer choice, as a fashionable cause.

As Dean continues, such formatting is premised 'on the exclusion of collective approaches to systemic problems'. The challenge for communists is to replace these individualized and fetishistic responses to environmental crisis with collective action against capitalism.

It cannot be denied that the left-wing media often articulate valuable environmental critiques. Following the Deepwater Horizon oil spillage, *The Guardian*'s John Vidal (28 May 2010) pointed out that BP could probably have avoided bad publicity if the disaster had occurred elsewhere, since:

…there are more than 2,000 major spillage sites in the Niger delta that have never been cleaned up; there are vast areas of the Columbian, Ecuadorian and Peruvian Amazon that have been devastated by spillages, the dumping of toxic materials and blowouts. Rivers and wells in Venezuela, Angola, Chad, Gabon, Equatorial Guinea, Uganda and Sudan have been badly polluted [...] The only reason oil costs $70-$100 a barrel today, and not $200, is because the industry has managed to pass on the real costs of extracting the oil.

The Guardian's George Monbiot (29 September 2009), meanwhile – one of the most incisive environmental journalists – dismisses plans hatched by a billionaire's club to curb population growth on environmental grounds, noting that it is the rich rather than the poor who despoil the environment most comprehensively. Another report in *The Guardian* (31 March 2010) cites evidence from the environmental campaign group Greenpeace showing that an oil company had funded an anti-environmentalist group. What even *The Guardian*'s journalists cannot concede, however, is that since the competitive forces driving environmental devastation are inherent to the capitalist mode of production, it is the system itself that must be destroyed.

On the contrary, the 'progressive' media tend to foster deep illusions about the redemptive possibilities of 'green capitalism'. Writing in *New Statesman* (21 June 2010) about the prospects for international environmental co-operation, the leftist environmental activist Bibi van der Zee argues that:

> ...the US and Chinese negotiating teams are made up of those who take the same approach to Mother Earth as a record company takes to a young band starting up: how can we milk this for maximum profit? It's pointless to hope we can make these people more cuddly – we can't. How can we make it financially imperative for them to get real? Some proper strategic thinking, please, so that we can get this army all fighting the same enemy.

Van der Zee is quite right to note that the ruling class will exploit the environment for profit to the fullest extent possible; but she is surely misguided in her hope that national bourgeoisies can unite to solve environmental problems. The failure of the 2009 Copenhagen environmental summit to even begin to tackle the problem of global warming – a failure acknowledged even by many mainstream journalists – suggests the untenability of this position. Global co-operation to solve human problems is impossible in a system based upon exploitation and international competition for profit. For all their faults, conservative commentators are often clearer on this point than their liberal counterparts. Despite holding a range of dubious enviro-sceptical views, the conservative columnist Dominic Lawson, for example, has rightly pointed out in his articles for *The Independent* that the profit motive is ultimately incompatible with serious environmental action.

The impossibility of a truly 'green capitalism' is further indicated by the protectionist responses of capitalist states to the threats posed by the escalating environmental crisis. A secret Pentagon report obtained by *The Observer* newspaper in 2004 warned that climate change had the potential to wreak global environmental catastrophe within decades, concluding that the issue should 'be elevated beyond a scientific debate to a national security concern'. Clearly, while the capitalist state perceives the peril of environmental destruction, it processes this menace not as a challenge facing humanity and requiring international co-operation, but as a threat to the security of the nation state, which must in turn prepare for struggles with other nations over the world's dwindling natural resources. Already the post-Cold War notion of a multi-polar world has acquired a dismal double meaning as the melting ice cap at the North Pole leads to bitter struggles between Canada, Russia, the US, Denmark and Norway, all of whom have made claims to the underlying seabed, which is suspected of containing vast quantities of undiscovered oil and gas. There is keen competition, too, over the ownership and control of the new shipping routes created by the thawing ice.

Bibi van der Zee's seemingly pragmatic call to find ways of spurring the ruling class into action thus misses the point that capitalism cannot muster the concerted action required to avert climate change. 'Getting real' about the environment requires us not to incentivise the ruling class, but to abolish it, while struggling to create a new society in which the chaos and waste of competitive capitalist production is replaced with the collective and organised production of goods and services aimed at satisfying human need rather than increasing profit. In this sense, we can readily agree with Al Gore that in order to survive as a species we must 'change the way [we] live' – albeit in a more radical way than Gore proposes.

The time available to effect this change, however, is limited. In order to restore the conditions for capital accumulation in increasingly difficult conditions, capitalism more and more resorts to the destruction of value – whether in the form of human life, infrastructure or the natural environment. Indeed, the effects of climate change and other environmental damage cannot be separated from capitalism's other ravages. In 2010, a large area of Pakistan was devastated by severe flooding whose onset seemed to confirm scientific warnings about the links between global warming and the increased incidence of intense rainfall; yet many of those affected were already suffering from the effects of dire poverty as well as the state's ongoing war against the Taliban and US drone attacks. The floods also provided a valuable opportunity for the Taliban – the only organisation distributing aid to many flood victims – to gain new recruits to its cause. As Naomi Klein notes in *The Shock Doctrine*, capitalism's disasters concatenate, so that a profits-oriented economic system, 'while bucking almost all serious attempts at environmental regulation, generates a steady stream of disasters [...], whether military, ecological, or financial'. Day by day, these disasters are also jeopardising the potential for the communist transformation of the planet. In the meantime, it is not the discredited enviro-scepticism of the conservative right, but the liberal fantasy of 'green' capitalism that represents the most pernicious mystification of the environmental challenges we face today.

7

'The only honourable course': the media and 'humanitarian' war

And the best at war finally are those who preach peace –
Charles Bukowski, 'The Genius of the Crowd'

In the summer of 2009, Harry Patch died. Patch had been one of the last surviving British soldiers to have fought in the First World War, the experience of which, quite understandably, he refused to discuss for many decades afterwards. In Patch's view, the First World War was 'organised murder' in which both Germans and British soldiers needlessly died serving the interests of their rulers. In an interview with BBC Radio 4's *Today* programme in 2005, Patch averred that 'It wasn't worth it. If two governments can't agree, give them a rifle each and let them fight it out. Don't lose twenty thousand men. It isn't worth it'. Asked by the interviewer if 'the world' had learned anything from World War I, Patch starkly replied with reference to world leaders: 'No. They never learn'. Patch's comments reflect the working class principle of internationalist solidarity; they rightly imply that workers had no class interest in fighting in – and every reason to oppose – the twentieth century's world wars. Patch's intransigent opposition to imperialist war has been applauded by some: the rock group Radiohead, for example, penned an anti-war song based on Patch's *Today* interview. Yet following Patch's death, all of the British news channels broadcast comments from, *inter alia*, the Queen, Prince Charles and the Prime Minister Gordon Brown, who – ignoring Patch's view of war – lost no time in claiming Patch as a symbol of noble 'sacrifice' for the nation.

A few months later, in a *BBC News at Ten* broadcast (3 March 2010), a variety of dignitaries registered their respect for the recently deceased left-wing Labour politician Michael Foot. The Prime Minister Gordon Brown noted Foot's 'commitment to justice' and praised the politician as 'good, compassionate, and dedicated to his country'. The last of these three accolades, at least, was beyond doubt. Amongst his many patriotic gestures, Foot, as co-author of the 1940 book *Guilty Men*, criticised the so-called 'appeasement' of German imperialism in the lead-up to the Second World War and supported Britain's entry into the war. Four decades later, Foot was a key player in the decision to send the British Task Force to the Falkland Islands in 1982, congratulating the Conservative Prime Minister Margaret Thatcher on her subsequent 'victory' (one that resulted in the deaths of large numbers of Argentine conscripts, many of them only teenagers). Foot was also an early advocate of the bombing of Serbia in the 1990s.

The media reports of each of these two men's lives and beliefs involved a staggering inversion of reality: the working class internationalist who had repeatedly stated his horror at the inhumanity of war and expressed international solidarity with 'enemy' combatants was posthumously claimed as a patriot who sacrificed his life for 'his' country. A nationalist, war-mongering politician, on the other hand, was honoured as a 'man of peace'. Taken together, these reports demonstrate the capitalist media's awesome capacity to recuperate working class political perspectives and to camouflage support for imperialist violence with the liberal language of 'peace' and humanitarianism.

Imperialist conflict has characterised capitalism since the beginning of the twentieth century. With the outbreak of the First World War in 1914, every aspect of social life was subsumed under the 'national interest' and every combatant state justified its entry into the war as a matter of national defence, demonising the enemy in the process. Writing about anti-German propaganda at the time, the British social critic Norman Angell, in his essay 'The Commercialization of Demagogy', noted with dismay that 'every story about the wickedness of Germans, [...] every cartoon revealing the Hun as a sly and fraudulent debtor, means crystallizing certain opinions, the stiffening of a certain attitude on social questions'. During both world wars, indeed, the press and later radio and newsreel films played an important role in justifying imperialist aggression. Indeed, the media continue to justify these world wars retrospectively, asserting the moral pre-eminence of 'our' nation state. Every schoolchild knows, for instance, that Britain and its allies fought on the side of 'good' against the 'evil' Nazis in the Second World War. Innumerable television documentaries about Hitler and the Schutzstaffel remind us of the horrors of the Nazi genocide – and rightly so. Yet the British terror in colonial India, or the British-engineered Bengal famine, which killed many millions of people during the Second World War (and possibly 30 million over the entire period of British rule, since the British, in India as in Ireland, used famine as a disciplinary tool) are seldom considered suitable topics for television documentaries; nor, for that matter, are the allied nuclear attacks on Japan or the terror bombings of German cities. To draw a more contemporary comparison: the six million slaughtered by the Nazis in the 1940s must 'never be forgotten'; but the six million slaughtered since the mid-1990s by armies supported by the Western powers in the Democratic Republic of Congo do not even register on the news agenda. Genocide is endemic to capitalism – but only 'their' genocides are recognised and memorialized by the media.

As the lionisation of Michael Foot shows, left-wing defences of imperialism often garner public support more effectively than crude jingoism. In the post-Cold War era, imperialist wars have increasingly been justified as 'humanitarian interventions', not just by conservative commentators, but also – and perhaps even more vociferously – by liberal journalists and academics. The inter-imperialist nature of the 1992-1995 Bosnian war, for example, has been buried underneath what Edward Herman and David Peterson have called the Western media's 'tsunami of lies and misrepresentations' as the conflict came to be framed as a Manichean struggle between the forces of good ('the West') and evil (the Serbs). The Western media's framing of the Bosnian war is highly instructive, in fact, as it set the precedent for the media coverage of NATO's 1999 bombing war against Slobodan Milošević's Yugoslavia and the US's more recent military assaults – also launched under the sacred banner of 'human rights' – upon Afghanistan and Iraq.

Accounts of the Bosnian war often omit any discussion of the conflict's origins in imperialist confrontation. As the Yugoslav regime disintegrated at the end of the Cold War, Muslim, Croat and Serb political parties competed in multi-party elections, fracturing the country along ethnic lines. Yet Yugoslavia's disintegration was also promoted by the Western powers. The German government rushed to extend full recognition to Croatia and as ethnic violence broke out between Serbs, Croats and Muslims, the US ultimately identified its own client through which to exert its influence in the region, aggressively promoting the 'independence' of Bosnia and backing the Muslims led by Alija Izetbegović (a Muslim fundamentalist and a member of a group that collaborated with the Nazi Schutzstaffel during the Second World War, committing atrocities against Jews and the resistance movement). As the Yugoslav region that had shown the greatest resistance both to an IMF-led austerity programmes imposed on Yugoslavia in the 1980s – and to the war when it began – Serbia was to be punished.

All sides involved in the Bosnian conflict committed appalling atrocities, burning villages and slaughtering and raping their populations. Yet the US media effectively recognised only one aggressor, instituting a relentless anti-Serb propaganda campaign. As the group No War But the Class War claims in its article 'Notes Towards a Text on the 1999 Balkan War and the Media':

> An article from a former soldier in Bosnia said that when an American TV crew turned up at his base they asked to see a burnt-out village previously inhabited by Bosnian Muslims – which they were duly shown. When the UN soldiers asked if they wanted to take photos of a burnt-out village previously inhabited by Bosnian Serbs, the journalists refused, saying it would confuse the issue: their viewers wanted clear ideas about what was going on.

Liberal journalists and intellectuals clamouring for military 'intervention' advanced their own 'clear ideas' about what to do with the Serbs. Anthony Lewis wrote *New York Times* columns demanding military action. Susan Sontag – mother of one of the chief journalist-apologists for the US invasion, David Rieff – and the actress Vanessa Redgrave made pilgrimages to Sarajevo to support imperialist violence. Indeed, the 'Bosnian question' flushed out numerous liberal academics and high-profile pundits as apologists for imperialism, most notably Christopher Hitchens, Michael Ignatieff, Todd Gitlin and Vaclav Havel. The nationalist frenzy that gripped liberals during the 1990s is epitomized by Richard Rorty's angry call, in *Achieving our Country*, for a left version of American patriotism. Not for nothing has Noam Chomsky identified the 1990s as the 'nadir' of recent Western intellectual history.

Britain, like most of the European states, had relatively little economic interest in the Balkans and its ruling class was divided over whether to orient itself towards Serbia or Croatia and over whether, during a recession, to undertake a costly military action. Ultimately, however, Britain accepted the position of the US as the latter developed a more aggressive policy towards Bosnia and the British media, like its US counterpart, began to adopt an anti-Serb position. One of the most hard-line interventionist newspapers throughout the 1990s was the liberal newspaper *The Independent*, whose journalists wrote of Serbian genocide and rape camps – accusations with no credible evidential basis, as Diana Johnson's book *Fools' Crusade* and Edward Herman and David Peterson's *Monthly Review* article 'The Dismantling of Yugoslavia' point out. The death camps rumour was circulated by a Croat public relations agency Ruder Finn in order to galvanise the support of Jewish pressure groups, which might otherwise have been less than enthusiastic to back the cause of Muslim fundamentalists with historical connections to the Nazis. Michael Parenti records in his book *To Kill A Nation: The Attack on Yugoslavia* that Ruder Finn's director, when challenged on the evidential basis of the company's claims, stated: 'Our work is not to verify information […] Our work is to accelerate the circulation of information favourable to us […] We had a job to do and we did it. We are not paid to moralize'. Meanwhile, from left to right, the British press, including *The Independent*, *The Telegraph*, *New Statesman*, *The Guardian* and *The Sun*, mobilised a range of racist stereotypes which demonised Serbs as tribal, primitive, evil, bloodthirsty and bestial, as the work of Philip Hammond has shown.

Adding insult to injury, the bias of Western journalists was justified by an appeal to a set of professional practices that collectively became known as the 'journalism of attachment': an allegedly new mode of affective reportage intended to cut through the suffocating 'neutrality' of existing journalism with a proper sense of moral outrage. The concept of the 'journalism of attachment' allowed liberal journalists such as Ed Vulliamy to present themselves as mavericks unafraid of 'speaking out' bravely and passionately about the horrors of war, while in practice doing so only on behalf of Muslim victims. In reality, these 'mavericks' constituted the journalistic mainstream and those who questioned their distortions, as Tariq Ali notes in the introduction to his collection *Masters of the Universe: NATO's Balkan Crusade*, 'were denounced as traitors, appeasers and worse'. Indeed, *contra* those journalists and academics who argued that media coverage of Bosnia was ineffectually neutral, British media coverage of the war was savagely partisan.

Advocates of Western 'intervention' in Bosnia (in fact, Western powers were heavily involved in Bosnia from the outset) were spectacularly rewarded in the autumn of 1995 when US warplanes attacked Bosnian Serb positions in Operation Storm. Towns and villages throughout Bosnia were targeted and many hundreds of civilians were killed and wounded. The US president Bill Clinton invoked Serbian human rights violations – comparing them to those committed by the Nazis during the Holocaust – to justify the operation. The bombings allowed the regular army of Croatia, together with Bosnian Muslim and Croat forces, to overrun Serb regions in northwest Bosnia in a ground offensive that killed and wounded thousands and turned another 125,000 people into refugees. They joined the quarter of a million Serb civilians driven out of Krajina by the Croatian army in what was, as Herman and Peterson point out, probably the war's largest single act of ethnic expulsion. Yet the suffering of the Serb population elicited no sympathy from those demanding 'humanitarian intervention' in Bosnia, since Operation Storm was what Herman and Peterson acerbically describe as 'benign' ethnic cleansing – that is, ethnic cleansing conducted by the US and its allies.

The media coverage of the notorious massacre of Muslims at the Bosnian town of Srebrenica, a UN 'safe haven', further illustrates the bias of the Western media reporting of the Bosnian war. Serb forces in and around Srebrenica committed appalling atrocities. Yet Western journalists took care to detach the massacre from its surrounding context. In 1992, the Serbs had been driven out of Srebrenica and the years leading up to the massacre saw many attacks on nearby Serb towns. Indeed, Srebrenica was not

simply a 'safe haven' for civilians; it also functioned as a UN
cover for Bosnian Muslim military operations. Yet this context
was not supplied in media references to Srebrenica. In his review
essay 'Diana Johnstone on the Balkan Wars', Edward Herman
notes that

> it has been an absolute rule of Rieff et al./media reporting on
> the Bosnian conflict to present evidence of Serb violence *in
> vacuo*, suppressing evidence of prior violence against Serbs,
> thereby falsely suggesting that Serbs were never responding
> but only initiated violence (this applies to Vukovar, Mostar,
> Tuzla, Goražde, and many other towns).

It is likely that more civilians were killed during the US's
Operation Storm than died at Srebrenica; yet only Srebrenica has
entered historical myth as 'genocide'. Herman and Peterson's
wider observation about the hypocrisy of US and British war
reporting is relevant here:

> We find it interesting that in the West, the millions or more
> deaths from the 'sanctions of mass destruction' and the
> hundreds of thousands of Iraqi deaths that have followed the
> 2003 invasion are never presented as 'genocide' or events that
> we 'must never forget'. These deaths did not merit the indig-
> nation of Ed Vulliamy, David Rieff, Samantha Power, and the
> mainstream media. The driving out of 250,000 Serbs from
> Croatia, and killing several thousand of them, doesn't even
> rate the designation of 'ethnic cleansing', let alone genocide.
> [...] The 16,000 Serb civilians killed in Bosnia in 1992–95 are
> effectively disappeared, while the 31,000 Muslim civilians
> killed in the latter years are elevated to world class status as
> victims of genocide.

As this passage suggests, the bias of Western media coverage of the Bosnian war was obscured by appeals to the universalist notion of humanitarianism – a keyword in the lexicon of Western imperialism in the 1990s. The hypocrisy of these appeals was most notable in the liberal media of the period: NATO's bombing of Yugoslavia in 1999 was announced by such forthright headlines as *The Sun*'s 'Clobba Slobba: Our Boys Batter Butcher of Serbia' and the *Daily Star*'s 'Serbs You Right'; yet the same attack was sanctioned with a decidedly chivalrous flourish in a *Guardian* leader article (23 March 1999) as 'the only honourable course for Europe and America'.

The more recent invasion of Iraq in 2003 was characterised by significant strategic disagreement within the ruling classes of the 'coalition' countries and by greater public opposition to the war than had been mounted against intervention in Yugoslavia. Nonetheless, the mainstream media generally supported the Iraq war – a war in which one million Iraqis died and perhaps 4.5 million were displaced. In America, newscasters and embedded reporters at both Fox News and the more liberal CNN referred to US forces as 'liberators' and 'heroes'. In the UK, where the ruling class itself was more divided over whether to invade, *The Guardian*, no doubt mindful of the significant public opposition to the war, was circumspect about the invasion, but nonetheless accepted (6 February 2003) that Iraq must be made to 'disarm' itself of its 'weapons of mass destruction' – weapons now conceded not to have existed. On the eve of the invasion, Bill Neely noted in ITV's *News at Ten* (19 March 2003) that 'the marines are prepared for one of the first and most daring operations'. The BBC was also robust in its support for the invasion. As David Edwards and David Cromwell document in their book *Guardians of Power: The Myth of the Liberal Media*, BBC journalists including Matt Frei, Andrew Marr, Rageh Omaar and John Simpson breathlessly endorsed the invasion – an invasion still seen by the BBC as, in the words of a Radio 4 lunchtime news broadcast (22 August 2010), 'the battle for a better Iraq'. In fact, despite the government's criticism of the BBC in the Hutton Report and inevitable allegations from the BBC's rivals in the conservative press that the organisation was 'anti-war', a Cardiff University study showed that the BBC was actually the *least* anti-war of the British news networks during the conflict, quoting more coalition sources and fewer Iraqi sources than the other networks and placing the least emphasis on Iraqi casualties. The BBC's support for the invasion was echoed by a roll call of elite liberal print journalists – the 'herd of independent minds', in Harold Rosenberg's phrase – including Nick Cohen, David Aaronovitch and Johann Hari. It would be churlish not to applaud the decency of those journalists – notably Omaar and Hari – who have rescinded their support for the war in recent years; yet here again we must be wary of the potential of such apologetics to humanise – and thereby restore public trust in – the capitalist media apparatuses and, by extension, the political institutions whose values they reflect.

The British media has been overwhelmingly supportive of the coalition's 'war on terror' in Afghanistan, often on humanitarian grounds. For example, Yasmin Alibhai-Brown – another journalist who later withdrew her support for war – voiced the widespread liberal opinion that the invasion was necessary to safeguard the human rights of Afghan women. In reality, however, the invasion of Afghanistan has led to appalling civilian suffering through drone attacks, bombing and other forms of terrorism. This misery has attracted little media interest at home. According to the news media watchdog Medialens, for example, the British media downplayed a report from Afghan government investigators that Special Forces executed ten Afghan civilians, eight of them children, in Kunar province during a joint US-Afghan operation on 27 December 2009. Stephen White of *The Mirror* ('Base Blast Kills Eight US civilians', 31 December 2009) ignored the story, reporting instead on the deaths of American civilians in a suicide bombing at an Afghan military base, while

The Sunday Telegraph (3 January 2010) described the incident as 'a raid in which US forces shot dead 10 people at a suspected bomb factory'. *The Guardian* (2 January 2010) relegated the story to a few lines at the end of a report on the death of a British bomb disposal expert, while BBC, ITN and Channel 4 television news made no mention of the incident. In fact, only Jerome Starkey of *The Times* (31 December 2009) reported the story. As Jake Lynch and Annabel McGoldrick suggest in 'How to improve war reporting in Afghanistan', 'the human cost of war in Afghanistan is being systematically downplayed', while 'the voices of Afghan people themselves are nearly always excluded'. Not only has the liberal media effectively condoned the devastation of Afghanistan, but the country's appallingly high rates of maternal deaths, violence against and enslavement of girls and women serve as a shocking refutation of the liberal myth that the war, which has now spilled over into Pakistan, was fought for women's liberation.

The news media's complicity with the coalition's recent wars has been complemented by sympathetic television documentaries about the experiences of the armed forces. The Ministry of Defence-approved Sky1 documentary *Ross Kemp in Afghanistan* (2008) and its sequel follow the daily lives of British troops in Afghanistan from the perspective of the soldiers. The youth channel BBC3, meanwhile, has done its bit for army recruitment and pro-war propaganda with *Girls on the Frontline* (25 March 2010). *Girls on the Frontline* offers a gender-specific reworking of the reality documentary series about US soldiers in Afghanistan, *Profiles from the Front Line* (ABC, 2003), which was based on a concept pitched by Jerry Bruckheimer to the US Pentagon. Over a pounding musical soundtrack, the programme tracks a group of female British soldiers training to be despatched to Afghanistan's Helmand province and frequently mentions the risks that they face. Like liberal feature films from *The Deer Hunter* to *The Hurt Locker*, these programmes reverently catalogue the privations suffered by 'our' troops, eliding both the geopolitical manoeuvres that underpin capitalist wars and the suffering of the majority of their victims. Such soft propaganda helps to manufacture public consent for imperialist terror far more insidiously than the gung-ho patriotism of the right-wing media.

During World War I, the German communist Karl Liebknecht famously reminded workers that 'the main enemy is at home'. The precept is also well understood by the ruling class. As John Pilger has written in *New Statesman* (29 March 2010): 'Western war-states such as the US and Britain are threatened not by the Taliban or any other introverted tribesmen in faraway places, but by the anti-war instincts of their own citizens'. In the battle to overcome these instincts, the patriotic cheerleading of the news media certainly plays a key role; Erich Fromm's remark in *The Sane Society* that 'nationalism is our form of incest, is our idolatry, is our insanity' remains accurate more than fifty years later. But at least as influential as today's right-wing media jingoists are the liberal journalists and commentators who – dripping with soulfulness, in Ralph Miliband's phrase – justify imperialist wars in the name feminism, liberation and humanitarianism and who, when civilian blood flows too conspicuously, can always repent their 'errors of judgement'.

8

Bogeyman at the BBC: Nick Griffin, *Question Time* and the 'fascist threat'

And they're resurrecting Churchill – XTC, 'War Dance'

Liberal democracies promise their electorates an enticing array of political choices. Yet in their fundamental political commitments, the political parties are essentially identical with one another: Despite their disagreements over policy, all support nationalism, imperialist wars and immigration control; as capitalist parties, they could hardly do otherwise. In what some see as today's 'post-political' moment, the parliamentary parties differ not on the basis of any ideological difference, but merely on how best to manage or administer a capitalist social arrangement that is presented as the natural order of things.

While news and current affairs programming reflects this capitalist consensus, the illusion of political variety is a valuable thing. Accordingly, representatives of the parliamentary parties criticise one another in the media (Britain has recently joined other countries in staging televised pre-election candidate debates), each presenting her own party as more progressive than her rival's. By providing an arena for such debates, televised political discussion programmes such as *Newsnight* and *Question Time* play a crucial role in promoting a view of Britain as a thriving democracy in which diverse viewpoints can be expressed and debated. The reality, however, is that for all their considerable cultural cachet as platforms for open debate, these programmes systematically exclude proletarian political perspectives. While the parties heatedly debate their policies on imperialist war, immigration or wages, the legitimacy of a system based on war, immigration and wage labour is not to be questioned and alternatives to capitalism – if they are ever mentioned at all – are quickly denounced as absurdly utopian or unspeakably brutal.

Never was the role of the current affairs media in sustaining the myth of political pluralism more apparent than in the appearance of the 'fascist' British National Party leader Nick Griffin on BBC1's flagship live political discussion programme *Question Time* on 22 October 2009. Before the broadcast, the prospect of Griffin appearing on the programme provoked furious demonstrations by a congeries of liberals, Trotskyists and other anti-fascists outside BBC buildings. It also incensed the liberal media. In *The Independent*, Steve Richards called the BNP 'a bunch of fascist outsiders', while *The Guardian* warned that by inviting Griffin onto the *Question Time* panel, the BBC was running the risk of 'normalising' the BNP and of providing the party with its 'best-ever platform for its poisonous politics'. *The Guardian*'s assertion of the BNP's fundamental difference from the other parties was also expressed by a cross-section of parliamentary politicians (witness the embarrassment caused when this myth of difference is exposed, as in 2009, when the British National Party raised its slogan 'British Jobs for British Workers', a phrase which, while originated by the BNP, had been used two years previously by Labour's Gordon Brown). Griffin's appearance thus presented a golden propaganda opportunity – but not only, or even mainly, to the BNP. For both *The Guardian* and the political establishment, Griffin had become a highly serviceable scapegoat, for the designation of the BNP as a uniquely 'poisonous' party could now be used to divert public attention from the repressive practices and policies of the political mainstream.

Predictably enough, on the evening of Griffin's appearance, the *Question Time* studio was transformed into a bear pit in which the live audience – and by extension the viewer at home – was encouraged to jeer and mock the BNP bogeyman (the 'two minute hate' in George Orwell's novel *1984* provides a clichéd, but not inaccurate literary analogy here). *Question Time*'s presenter, David Dimbleby, under orders from BBC managers to put Griffin under pressure, relentlessly attacked Griffin, even asking him at one point why he was smiling. Griffin, as many commentators have pointed out, seemed ill at ease in the 'debate' and his racist and often preposterous arguments were easily countered and denounced. Yet the representatives of the other political parties on the panel managed to out-Griffin Griffin, vying to out-do one another with their tough lines on immigration. When Griffin claimed that his party was heir to the legacy of the genocidal imperialist Winston Churchill, the other panellists – each of them sporting the patriotic symbol of the red poppy on their lapels – quickly objected, only to claim the same distinction for themselves.

From the establishment's perspective, Griffin's appearance was highly successful. The audience had been given its pound of flesh, the BBC had got to look tough (thus placating at least some of those liberals who had feared that the broadcast might 'legitimise' the BNP) and the mainstream politicians had exploited the occasion for maximal advantage, parading their patriotic credentials. In the tabloid press, meanwhile, reports about Griffin's appearance took on a carnivalesque tone. On the day of the broadcast, *The Mirror*'s main feature article on the subject, entitled 'Question Slime', was accompanied by an unflattering photograph of Griffin and contained furious denunciations of the BNP leader written by a former commander of British troops in Afghanistan, Colonel Richard Kemp. Underneath the article, a scatological cartoon entitled 'Nick Griffin Gets Ready for Tonight's Show' showed Griffin aiming his posterior towards a microphone in the *Question Time* studio as a technician reassures him that the recording equipment 'should pick up everything you say'. Yet the knockabout triumphalism of the politicians and the tabloid press smacked more than a little of hypocrisy.

During the broadcast, Griffin's fellow panellist Labour's Jack Straw – who in 2006 denounced Muslim women who wear the niqab veil – proclaimed that his party, unlike the BNP, is guided by a 'moral compass'. Yet nobody who has read Robert Clough's *Labour: A Party Fit for Imperialism* can doubt that the Labour Party is a racist and imperialist political party of long standing. The most recent Labour government enforced a panoply of measures for violently controlling immigration and immigrants, such as dawn raids on the homes and workplaces of 'illegal' immigrants and undocumented workers, citizenship tests, detention, deportation and the violent dispersal of immigrants from makeshift camps by riot police. The BNP could only dream of implementing such oppressive measures, the human consequences of which can be appalling. Attempts by migrants to avoid detection by immigration officials, for example, often result in dangerous and sometimes lethal 'people trafficking'. To take just one example, when Labour's Jack Straw was Home Secretary in 2000, 58 Chinese migrants were found dead in a truck at Dover after they had been smuggled into the UK. In fact, despite Straw's abstract claim to ethical superiority over the BNP, Labour at the time of the *Question Time* broadcast was the more dangerously racist party, if only for the simple reason that it was in power and *actually implementing* oppressive anti-immigration policies. It should be added that Labour instigated the genocidal war on Iraq, which the BNP opposed.

Not everybody who denounces the BNP as a threat to democracy, of course, is as cynical as Jack Straw – and the BNP, like its rival in racism, the English Defence League, is clearly a malignant force. Yet scaremongering over such parties also serves to buttress the existing political order, often by raising the spectre of fascism. Chomsky and Herman's propaganda model posited 'anti-communism' as a news media 'filter'. Yet while communism retains its mythic threat long after the end of the Cold War,

Western powers also invoke the demons of historical fascism in order to boost their own credibility and justify their military 'interventions'. In the British news media today it could even be argued that fascism, rather than communism, has become the foremost 'anti-ideology' – that is, an ideology whose supposed threat to liberal values can be exploited in defence of the current power system.

However that may be, the widespread notion that the 'fascist' British National Party poses a threat to democracy rests on historical ignorance and political naivety. For one thing, in the years since fascism posed a real political threat, the term has undergone significant semantic weakening. Orwell noted this trend as early as 1946 in 'Politics and the English Language', while today, as Michael Hardt and Toni Negri observe at the beginning of their book *Commonwealth*, many leftists see signs of fascism wherever they look:

> Many refer to the U.S. government as fascist, most often citing Abu Ghraib, Guantanamo, Fallujah, and the Patriot Act. Others call the Israeli government fascist by referring to the continuing occupations of Gaza and the West Bank, the use of assassinations and bulldozers as diplomacy, and the bombing of Lebanon. Still others use 'islamofascism' to designate the theocratic governments and movements in the Muslim world.

The US and Israeli states, like 'Muslim' jihadists, are undoubtedly terroristic and brutal; yet, as Hardt and Negri point out, they are hardly fascist. The BNP, for its part, is a populist nationalist party rather than a fascist party in the sense that, say, the German National Socialists were in the 1930s and 40s, or other tiny parties in Britain, such as the British Federation of Fascists, are today. Fascism – the unification of capitalist economics and politics – was the response of specific national capitals to the organisational weaknesses of the state in the period following World War I; but it is hardly a useful mode of capitalist organisation under present conditions. Indeed, for as long as immigrant labour is profitable to capitalists, the BNP, in order to stand any hope of winning political power, would have to abandon those of its policies, such as repatriation, less congenial to the functioning of capitalist accumulation. In any event, it is highly questionable whether the proletariat has the power determine the form – democratic or fascist – that the capitalist state will take; as Gilles Dauvé starkly observes in his essay 'Fascism/Anti-Fascism', 'the political forms which capital gives itself do not depend on the actions of the working class'.

These historical and political considerations are conveniently overlooked by liberal anti-fascists. By invoking the threat of bogeymen such as Nick Griffin, anti-BNP campaigners reinforce the capitalist *status quo* while preserving their supposedly 'progressive' credentials. But, at the very least, those who campaign against the BNP ought to protest equally vociferously against the far more powerful, liberal factions of the state. Here Max Horkheimer's famous aphorism – 'he who does not wish to speak of capitalism, should also be silent about fascism' – seems as relevant today as it was in the middle of the twentieth century and perhaps even more so, given that fascism, especially in countries such as the UK and US, does not currently pose the threat it once did.

The exhibition of fascist bogeymen for propaganda purposes is neither new nor confined to the British and US contexts. Ever since the Second World War, the spectre of a fascist threat has been mobilised by the liberal media in order to rally the working class behind the 'defence of democracy'. It was a putatively socialist president of France, François Mitterand, for example, who insisted in the early 1980s that the anti-immigration politician Jean-Marie Le Pen be granted television and radio airtime. A lynchpin of capitalist ideology, anti-fascism even permeates fictional media forms: television dramas such as the

BBC's fawning Winston Churchill biopic *The Gathering Storm* (2004) and hip feature films such as Quentin Tarantino's anti-Nazi romp *Inglourious Basterds* (2009) all contribute to the belief that liberal capitalism, for all its faults, is preferable to fascism – a belief that may take some bolstering among the relatives of those massacred and maimed, from Dresden to Hiroshima, by the allied forces during the Second World War. In many democratic countries and across many forms of media, fascism has become the ultimate scapegoat for the horrors of capitalism.

Liberal academia plays its part here, too. In a *History Today* article about Nick Griffin's *Question Time* appearance, historian Gavin Schaffer traces the history of debates within the BBC about the extent to which it is appropriate to give airtime to 'racial extremism'. Schaffer's article is carefully researched, but its argument is all too comfortably aligned with the propaganda values of the BBC and the wider anti-fascist campaign of the British state. Schaffer argues enthymematically: designating parties such as the BNP as 'racial extremists', he implies that the views of 'mainstream' politicians are moderate and that their reiteration on the BBC's premier political discussion programme is unproblematic. But as suggested above, it is not difficult to demonstrate that Labour, the Conservatives and the other parliamentary political parties practice their own forms of 'racial extremism'.

Schaffer concludes his article by applauding the bravery of the BBC's decision to grant a platform to the BNP. The BBC today, he argues, 'maintain[s] its long-standing belief that it has a duty to present British society "warts and all" and does not have the right to suppress views that are odious but legal'. It is worth repeating here that *all* of the capitalist parties – not just the BNP – have policies on immigration that could be described as 'odious'. Moreover, Schaffer's endorsement of the notion that the BBC presents British society 'warts and all' accepts at face value the BBC's cherished self-image as an impartial political arbiter.

But the BBC has never been a neutral organisation; on the contrary, its news and current affairs broadcasts systematically marginalise working class perspectives and viewpoints critical of the British state and its allies. From this perspective, Griffin's appearance on *Question Time* can be seen not as an index not of the BBC's long-standing commitment to neutrality, but as a confirmation of its age-old political biases. By parading Nick Griffin as a scapegoat in order to deflect attention from the oppressive immigration policies of the mainstream parties, the BBC once again proved its credentials as the servant of the British state – a role it has performed with impressive consistency since Reith offered his organisation's support to the British government during the 1926 General Strike.

The political and media exploitation of the BNP certainly did not begin in 2009. Mike Wayne and Craig Murray's recent research on British political television news broadcasting in May 2006 suggests that the BNP attracted far more attention than the minority left-wing Respect Party in that month's local elections, although both parties enjoyed a roughly equal level of electoral success, suggesting that the BNP was 'made visible precisely to underline that the mainstream parties constitute the only sensible political discourse'. A number of television documentaries, meanwhile, such as Sky's mocking and salacious *BNP Wives* (2008), have also kept anti-BNP sentiment running high in recent years. Yet the Griffin affair channelled these pre-existing currents into a high-profile political pantomime in a way that proved highly serviceable to the ruling class and the capitalist media. In the lead-up to the British general election in 2010, journalists were able to present the BNP as the dreaded Other, or 'constitutive outside', of bourgeois democracy and thus to frame the election as a contest between the legitimate agents of 'democratic' freedom and the dark forces of fascist tyranny. On a Radio 4 news item about the election (14 April 2010), for example, the BBC reporter James Landale wondered: 'can the BNP win a breakthrough, or can the other parties keep them out?' – a question he repeated in the BBC's *10 O'Clock News* television bulletin on the same evening. For working class people, however, the predication of political freedom on a choice between the 'fascist' parties and their democratic counterparts, like anti-fascist discourse in general, constitutes a dangerous mystification of political reality.

9

'Thus far and no further': *New Statesman* and the limits of critique

If the system functions well, it ought to have a liberal bias, or at least appear to. Because if it appears to have a liberal bias, that will serve to bound thought even more effectively – Noam Chomsky, interview, in *Manufacturing Consent: Noam Chomsky and the Media*

It is fashionable among British liberal media critics to deride the conservative views of the US television channel Fox News or the right-wing newspapers *The Daily Mail* and *Daily Express*, while defending the supposedly more liberal, public service news organisations such as the BBC (and, in the US, CNN). Yet as this book has repeatedly shown, the BBC, along with the left-liberal press, also consistently supports capitalist agendas, often with considerable subtlety. The point can be clarified through a brief consideration of the ideological orientation of the most influential left-wing political magazine in the UK: *New Statesman*.

As Raymond Kuhn points out in his book *Politics and the Media in Britain*, political and current affairs magazines are less popular in Britain than in some other countries, such as the US, Germany and France (as evidenced by the high sales of *Newsweek*, *Der Spiegel* and *Le Nouvel Observateur* in those countries), not least because of the relatively high level of newspaper readership in Britain. Yet modest as its circulation may be, *New Statesman* occupies a distinguished position as the guiding voice of the political and intellectual left in Britain.

While television broadcasters are obliged to maintain party political impartiality, the editorial politics of British newspapers and magazines are normally aligned with one of the political parties. Since its first publication in 1913, *New Statesman* has supported the Labour Party, initially for the reason that the Labour was a socialist party and more recently on the less ambitious grounds that Labour is at least more 'progressive' than its rivals. As Neal Lawson, director of the Labour-supporting pressure group Compass, asserted in *New Statesman* (3 May 2010) in the run-up to the 2010 general election: 'Labour remains the crucial vehicle for progressive hopes'. Analysing the defeat of Labour at the election a few weeks later (31 May 2010), *New Statesman* contributors Jonathan Rutherford and John Cruddas – the latter is a politician associated with the left wing of the Labour Party, who is now flirting with nationalist populism as part of the 'Blue Labour' movement – opined that Labour, while remaining the 'progressive' party, had lost because it had failed to convince working people of its 'core values' of 'freedom and democracy'. But given the Labour Party's support for both of the twentieth century's imperialist world slaughters (and many more besides) and its long history of violently repressing working class militancy, promoting Labour as a 'progressive' party committed to 'freedom and democracy' is no easy task.

New Statesman writers regularly excuse Labour's support for the most egregious of atrocities as political lapses or aberrations. As a panellist on the BBC's Sunday morning discussion programme *The Big Questions* (27 June 2010), *New Statesman*'s senior editor Mehdi Hasan keenly denounced atrocities committed by allied troops in Afghanistan and advocated troop withdrawal. Tellingly, at the time of the broadcast, a Conservative government was in power. Yet only a month earlier, in a BBC *Question Time* appearance under a *Labour* government (13 May 2010), a more subdued Hasan had understatedly called Labour's genocidal adventure in Iraq a 'stain on its record' (compare the Labour leader Ed Miliband's prim phrase 'a profound mistake'). In truth, the Labour Party's prosecution of the Iraq war amply demonstrated its imperialist credentials; yet *New Statesman* generously excuses such attacks as errors from which lessons must be learned – until the next war, of course.

New Statesman occasionally publishes politically radical articles: John Pilger regularly critiques the delusions and deceptions of Western *realpolitik*, while Laurie Penny has written many commendable articles, questioning, for example, the nationalistic and militaristic connotations of the red poppy worn in Britain on Remembrance Day and defending the reputation of the British student anti-cuts protestors in 2010, after they were widely smeared in the media as violent hooligans. Even in *New Statesman*, however, radical critique is the preserve of just one or two contributors. Moreover, criticisms of exploitation or of national borders – that is, of the fundamental elements of the capitalist order – are off limits. Notwithstanding the spirited broadsides of Pilger and Penny, *New Statesman*'s editorial line is reformist rather than radical, endorsing parliamentary politics and supporting the left wing of the capitalist political apparatus.

One of the elements that makes *New Statesman* such an effective instrument of capitalist propaganda is its readiness to flirt with radical perspectives and criticisms. In an essay (29 March 2010) lauding the value of voluntary organisations, for example, Geoffrey Wheatcroft attacks the welfare state for creating a 'permanent underclass'. Wheatcroft notes some arresting facts, reminding us that 'there are council estates in east Glasgow where life expectancy is now lower than in Bangladesh'. But he does not see such facts as consequences of an inhuman political system; instead, he relates poor living conditions to the 'culture' of state dependency supposedly promoted by post-war Keynesianism. Wheatcroft hastily dismisses socialism, meanwhile, by equating it with the reactionary ideologies of Fabianism and Stalinism (ironically, it was the Fabians Beatrice and Sydney Webb who established *New Statesman* in 1913 and in the 1930s the magazine, like other left-wing elements at the time, eulogised Stalin). The essay concludes with an attack on the 'foreign' ownership of Chelsea football club and a panegyric to 'patriotic pride' in an age in which 'many of us more often feel shame about our country than its opposite'. Disjointed as Wheatcroft's article is, its ideological support for the interests of the national capital and its smearing of radical politics by association with Stalinism constitute the staple elements of *New Statesman*'s political discourse and consolidate the magazine's status as a 'loyal opposition' whose radical posturing conceals a consistent and uncompromising defence of the capitalist nation state.

The magazine's perspective on foreign politics is no less problematic, as a brief consideration of two articles in the same edition of *New Statesman* (28 June 2010) will serve to indicate. Both articles deal with leftist icons. The first is *Independent* journalist Peter Popham's hagiographic portrait of the Burmese politician Aung San Suu Kyi, a social democrat and daughter of the British-installed ex-Prime Minister of Burma (Myanmar), Aung San. When Popham's article was written, Aung San Suu Kyi had been placed under house arrest by the ruling Burmese junta, which is heavily under the influence of China. Winner of the Nobel peace prize in 1991, she has become a key focus of Western imperial ambition in Burma and the poster girl of 'pro-democracy' activists. Popham praises Aung San Suu Kyi's stead-fastness, calling her 'Suu the Unyielding', and frequently alludes to her glamorous and youthful appearance.

Yet the article's sexism is less troubling than its support for Aung San Suu Kyi's nationalism. Titled 'Her nation's best hope', the article presents the politician as a saintly pro-democratic celebrity waiting to step into the political limelight, while Burma's intellectuals, workers and peasants secretly clutch photographs of their heroine and passively wait for her party to rescue the country. Aung San Suu Kyi's opposition party, the National League for Democracy, is indeed seen by Western states as the 'best hope' of gaining political leverage and curtailing the influence of Chinese imperialism in the region. Although British and US capital investment in Burma is significant, Western states have a clear interest in destabilising the pro-Chinese leadership of a state that is as rich in mineral and gas deposits as it is in geo-strategic potential. Yet Popham's article overlooks such material considerations. In common with the BBC Radio 4 documentary about Aung San Suu Kyi, *Freedom from Fear* (18 June 2010) and the welter of fawning Western media tributes to Aung San Suu Kyi that followed her release from house arrest in November 2010, Popham's article serves as a puff piece for the West's preferred dictator-in-waiting.

A second *New Statesman* article from 28 June 2010, Noam Chomsky's 'Another world is possible', discusses the prospects for 'democracy' in Latin America. Chomsky's piece, which is an extract from his book *Hopes and Prospects*, points to the popularity of leaders like the self-styled 'market socialist' Hugo Chávez in Venezuela, hinting vaguely that in both Bolivia and Venezuela there are 'vibrant popular organisations' and a sense of 'real participation' in social decision-making. Unlike Popham's article, which eulogises a potential Western ally, Chomsky, in praising Chávez, lends his support to a politician whose regime is already in power and which poses a significant challenge to the ambitions of US imperialism (herein lies the attraction of Chávismo for 'progressives' and leftists). Like many of those who make up the left wing of capitalism – from liberals to Trotsykists – Chomsky appears to endorse the Chávist propaganda of the new 'Bolivarian revolution', along with its notion that left-wing factions of the state can engineer a 'socialist' consensus between workers and capitalists.

Yet as the International Communist Current, a group that has frequently documented the oppressions of the Chávez regime over the last decade, points out in an online article in 2008, 'the state has been in the hands of the Chávists since 1999, but has not magically lost its capitalist character'. Indeed, the stark realities of class conflict in Venezuela confound Chomsky's optimistic analysis. In March 2008, to take just one example, the Venezuelan state launched a furious attack on striking steel workers, arresting and injuring many of them. Indeed, while Chomsky's article counterposes the democratic wave represented by Chávez's nationalist populism to the depredations of 'free market' neoliberalism, evidence about daily life from workers' groups in Venezuela paints a grim picture of life in the country. In their article 'The revolution delayed: 10 years of Hugo Chávez's rule', Charles Reeve and members of the Caracas-based journal *El Libertario* discuss how Chávez has implemented neoliberal 'reforms' and attacked workers' rights. Thousands of oil workers have been sacked and average wages and living standards are falling as working class jobs are casualised. State repression of political dissent is brutal and political discrimination is rife: to obtain employment in the public sector, for example, workers must express allegiance to Chávez and are forced to participate in pro-regime marches. The 'popular organisations' to which Chomsky approvingly refers, meanwhile, presumably include the community councils which, like their Cuban counterparts, merely impose state surveillance at street level. Membership of both community and factory councils depends on strict obedience to the Partido Socialista Unido de Venezuela. As the communist Internationalist Perspectives group summarises in its article 'Venezuela and the "Bolivarian Revolution"': 'the "grass-roots organizations" [...] have mostly served to preserve social peace and to consolidate the new state power'. Some indication of Chávez's moral character, meanwhile, may be gleaned from the company the president keeps. Chávez calls his ally, the Holocaust-denying Iranian President Mahmoud Ahmadinejad, his 'revolutionary brother' and admires the bloodthirsty former Ugandan dictator Idi Amin as a 'patriot'.

What, then, are we to make of Chomsky's apologetics for

Chávez? Chomsky is undoubtedly one of the pre-eminent critics of US imperialism and his rigorous analyses of US media propaganda show a lucid understanding of the relationship between the media and ruling class interests. But the radical perspective of Chomsky's critique of the media is inconsistent with the statism of his concrete political attachments, another example of which is Chomsky's endorsement of a 'two-state' solution to the Israel-Palestine conflict (although Chomsky does at least acknowledge that a 'no state' solution to the conflict is ultimately preferable). As contributors to *El Libertario* have pointed out, Chomsky's support for Chávez contradicts his avowedly 'anarchist-libertarian' principles. After all, Venezuela is assuredly a capitalist state. As Rosa Luxemburg argued long ago, imperialist policy is not the creation of one country or group of countries, but the expression of a particular stage of global capitalist development from whose determinations no state is immune. Moreover, even if one were to argue, through some feat of ideological gymnastics, that the Chávez regime is counteracting neoliberalism, the task of radicals, as Chris Wright remarks in a critique of David Harvey's work on this subject, 'is not to defeat neoliberalism or any other model of accumulation, but to deny accumulation itself'.

The prospect of publishing an article written by Noam Chomsky is an enticing one for a magazine with pretensions to radicalism. But Chomsky's political positions are hardly communist in nature and *New Statesman*'s publication of Chomsky's most statist arguments ensures that the magazine's political critique does not stray beyond the ideological limits of liberalism. It is worth remembering here that selective 'anti-imperialist' critiques of the US or Israel, such as those made by Chomsky – and, for that matter, by Chávez – are by no means unacceptable to all elements of the British establishment; after all, while Britain's economic and military interests are often tied to those of the superpower, Britain is not merely a 'poodle' of the

10

Beyond the news: popular culture against the working class

TV say if you're poor, you must be slow and shiftless / But you pay 'em to say that so we don't want it different – The Coup, 'Lazymuthafucka'

This book has been concerned with the propaganda function of contemporary news and current affairs media. Needless to say, however, the dissemination of state propaganda is not restricted to these formats. On British television, for example, references to the Help for Heroes charity – which has strong ties to the state and military apparatuses – have turned up in myriad entertainment programmes, from the reality television spin-off *The Apprentice – You're Fired* to the soap opera *EastEnders*. Yet popular media formats sustain capitalist hegemony in less egregious ways, too. A brief consideration of some of the themes and concerns of contemporary lifestyle and reality television will help to illustrate how class-based discourses are diffused through popular culture.

Gilles Deleuze proposed that developed capitalist societies transitioned in the course of the twentieth century from 'disciplinary societies', in which capitalists manage workers through physical discipline and institutions, to 'societies of control', in which individuals voluntarily internalise the values and interests of their rulers as their own. In the society of control, the media – and in particular the 'domestic' medium of television – play a major role in constituting us as capitalist subjects by manufacturing a social consensus based on bourgeois values. In 1962, in the wake of the Pilkington Report into the quality of British television, Raymond Williams noted in his article 'Television in Britain' that 'majority television' was 'outstandingly an expression of the false consciousness of our particular societies'. Williams' judgement remains eminently applicable to popular television today. In *The Apprentice*, contestants compete against one another for an internship with a business mogul, while in *Dragon's Den* and *High Street Dreams*, ordinary members of the public seek to impress businesspeople and financiers with their entrepreneurial acumen. Other programmes fetishize the acquisition of houses ('properties', in lifestyle television discourse) and property speculation, while television programmes about obesity, exercise, cosmetic surgery and dieting encourage viewers to focus their attentions on their personal well-being and appearance. Indeed, the proliferation of 'transformational' reality television programmes in recent years – from home improvement shows to makeover programmes – reflects and reinforces a profound investment in disciplinary work and biopolitical self-regulation. In such programmes, as Adorno observed of contemporary capitalist society in *Minima Moralia*, 'everybody must have projects all the time', so that 'the whole of life must look like a job'.

Such television programming also interpellates working class people as self-contained units of production and consumption, fostering what the Marxist writer Christopher Caudwell liked to call the 'bourgeois illusion' of individualism. Little wonder that so many people today believe that human beings are 'naturally' selfish – a proposition that has been refuted by scientists from Peter Kropotkin to Stephen Jay Gould – and that this supposed 'fact' precludes the possibility of communism. (It might be noted here that even if human nature *were* essentially characterised by selfishness, this would constitute an argument not *against* communism but *in favour* of it, since the fact of human selfishness would necessitate reciprocal social arrangements capable of preventing the exploitation of some human beings by others).

The entrenched individualism of many popular television programmes tends to vitiate any sense that the problems faced by working class people and communities can be overcome collectively. In each episode of Channel 4's reality programme *The Secret Millionaire*, an undercover millionaire encounters several community-minded individuals, each with their own project designed to help a disadvantaged group of people. At the end of the episode, the millionaire reveals her identity, writing a cheque for one or more of the deserving causes she has encountered. Here, as in Žižek's 'chocolate laxative' paradigm, capitalism is posited as the remedy for the very problems it has caused. Channel 4's *How the Other Half Live* operates on a similar premise: a wealthy family donates money to a poorer one, having first ensured that its members are deserving of support. In programmes such as these, working class people are urged to 'better themselves' through hard work. This in turn tends to deny agency to the working class *as a class*, implying that complex social problems can be rectified not by the collective action of the workers against their exploiters, but by a combination of individual effort and perhaps, for a lucky few, the *deus ex machina* of benevolent philanthropic intervention – a proposition that chimes with the emphasis placed upon private charity in the Cameronian one nation fantasy of the 'Big Society'. As for collectivity, we are left with the ersatz participation of the *X Factor* phone-in.

Yet the radical critique of 'reality', 'aspirational' and lifestyle television formats should in no way involve a moralistic objection to the enjoyment of wealth or 'middle class' comforts; after all, in contrast with the gloomy *ressentiment* and anti-consumerism of the left-liberal consensus, the communist demand is nothing if not a demand for *more*. The criticism is rather that lifestyle television's exhortations to social mobility and consumerism serve to occlude both the reality of exploitation and the potential for collective socio-political action.

They also disregard the increasing poverty of the working class. As the 'wealth gap' widens and social mobility rates flat-line, average wages and living standards for workers in 'developed' capitalist societies have stagnated or fallen in recent years, as even the capitalist news media are sometimes compelled to acknowledge: Neil Irwin of *The Washington Post*, for example, noted in an article in January 2010 that the net worth of American households fell throughout the first decade of the twenty-first century.

The increasingly fragile fantasy of upward mobility finds expression in many other popular media forms today. It is a convention of hip-hop videos, for example, to be set dually 'on the street' and 'at the mansion'. In the dream-like logic of the music video, celebrity rappers transition effortlessly between these two settings. Association with 'the street' allows even the most sybaritic celebrities to maintain a reputation as 'authentic', 'real' and 'cool'. The mythologisation of easy social advancement, meanwhile, furnishes an aspirational ideal while eliding the economic constraints that preclude social mobility for the majority of people in the real world. As such examples suggest – and as any advertising executive knows – capitalist hegemony is maintained not only through the assertion of nationalist symbolism and state propaganda, but also through the reconfiguration of human dreams, desires, aspirations and emotions.

As well as fostering an individualistic mindset, popular media often ridicule working class people who attain cultural prominence: witness the outpouring of class hatred in tabloid television's treatment of working class – especially female – 'chav' or 'white trash' celebrities, such as Jade Goody, Kerry Katona and Britney Spears, who are often censured for their emotional instability, stupidity, vulgarity, corpulence or maternal incompetence. It is precisely such undisciplined and recalcitrant working class people that the experts and gurus of 'rehab' reality television aim to instruct in the virtues of self-restraint and hard work. In BBC3's *Young, Dumb and Living Off Mum*, young working class individuals are mocked for their indolence and cajoled into taking low-paid, service sector jobs. In Channel 4's *Benefit Busters* and *The Fairy Jobmother*, meanwhile, presenter Hayley Taylor mobilises a mixture of moral censure and therapeutic rhetoric in an attempt to wean working class families 'off benefits' and 'into work' – as though unemployment were, to use the phrase of the Conservative Chancellor of the Exchequer George Osborne, a 'lifestyle choice'.

But it is perhaps in the treatment of crime that the anti-working class nature of these popular media formats is most evident. The police force is all but venerated in reality television documentaries, while working class criminals, from violent gangs to 'hoodies' and 'chavs' are excoriated in the news media and in television docusoaps such as Bravo channel's *Street Crime UK* and its replacement *Brit Cops*. And while largely juvenile, anti-social crime does constitute a genuine blight on society (one whose impact is felt most keenly in working class communities), what Marcuse termed 'the mature delinquency' of the ruling class – such as brutal invasions and bombings, lethal sanctions on food and medicines, health and safety violations – are either simply not classified as crimes or ignored; indeed, corporate and political crimes barely feature in crime-related television programming. Such evasions obscure the truth that the most pernicious and chronic threats to the well-being of working class people are posed not by other workers, but by what Žižek calls the 'objective' or systemic violence of capitalist social relations, which finds expression in work-related 'accidents', poverty, 'stress', environmental damage, genocide and warfare. But there's not much entertainment value in discussing any of that.

11

An ever-changing sameness: countering the myths of media pluralism

The flaw in the pluralist heaven is that the heavenly chorus sings with a strong upper-class accent – Elmer Eric Schattschneider, *The Semi-Sovereign People*

If the thesis of this book is that the left-wing media offers no serious alternative to the politics of the right, it remains to identify and attempt to rebut some of the potential objections to this argument. Writing in the early 1970s, the unjustly neglected media critic Herbert Schiller noted the widespread acceptance of the 'myth of media pluralism'. New life is breathed into this myth every time a liberal critic praises the contemporary media's exhaustiveness and diversity. But as this book has argued, the media reproduce the worldview of the ruling class with impressive consistency, despite the vast array of programme formats and genres across the enormously expanded range of media channels available today. We should resist the temptations of 'strong functionalism' here: the media do not always reflect the interests of the state *optimally* and journalists and other media practitioners may have their own ideas about what they are doing when they write articles or produce television news bulletins. But the fact remains that the capitalist media systematically tends to reflect the interests of its owners and controllers – the corporations and the capitalist state – so that mostly, as Chomsky writes in *Deterring Democracy*, 'what conflicts with the requirements of power and privilege does not exist'.

This does not mean that the capitalist media industries are sclerotic. On the contrary, there have been significant changes in the nature of news broadcasting in recent years, including the rise of 'soft', often heavily celebritised news, 'infotainment', and the replacement of professional reporting with 'raw testimonies of experience', as Graham Murdock has put it. The key point for communists, however, is not simply that the capitalist news media have become de-professionalised or 'dumbed down' (a perennial complaint about journalism – one thinks here of Matthew Arnold's attack upon the 'feather-brained' 'new journalism' of the late nineteenth century), but that they systematically exclude working class political perspectives.

Beyond the news, it is undeniable that a striking diversity of media genres and formats is available today. The last decade alone has seen the emergence in Britain of so-called 'lad mags', an explosion of reality television, and the development of myriad new media technologies. Media formats, genres, technologies and platforms emerge, converge – and sometimes disappear – with bewildering rapidity, as capitalists seek to develop products for niche audiences against a backdrop of falling profits and market saturation. Yet no matter how new or innovative the format may be, expressions of alternatives to the dominant ideology are vanishingly rare. A rapid turnover of new media products, formats and fashions hardly constitutes a challenge to capitalist ideology; on the contrary, as Fredric Jameson observes in *The Seeds of Time*, capitalism's restlessly changing phenomenal surface belies, at a deeper level, a social order that is more static than ever, Adorno's 'ever-changing sameness'.

Some may object that the news media, for all its faults, often brings to light political corruption by calling institutional power to account. To take a celebrated example, the exposure of the Watergate scandal is sometimes hailed as a triumph of American investigative reporting. Yet Watergate was elevated into a major political scandal because it afforded Nixon's political rivals a means to put pressure on his administration, whose foreign policy objective of ending the Vietnam war was failing (moreover, as Chomsky noted at the time in the *New York Review of Books*, what was scandalous about Watergate was that its targets were rich and powerful men rather than radical groups whose infiltration by the state is so routine that it attracts no media attention). Similarly, the Monica Lewinsky scandal that rocked the Clinton administration in 1998 surely had less to do with moral concerns about the US president's sexual antics than with Republican objections to his administration's controversial foreign policy orientation towards China rather than Japan. The Lewinsky scandal was thus not a bold journalistic exposé of presidential corruption, but a tawdry exercise in politically motivated mud-slinging.

Indeed, the ruling class is not homogenous and the media often stoke the internecine tensions within it on behalf of one or another of its cliques. In this sense, political scandals do not contest capitalist power so much as serve particular factions of it. In Britain, an investigation by the *Mail on Sunday* (5 July 2010) newspaper detailed the astronomical sums of money expended on the former Labour Prime Minister Tony Blair's holidays and business trips. The sums of money involved were indeed staggeringly large; yet the *Mail*'s support for the Conservative party suggests that the exposé was motivated by factional interest rather than a principled objection to Blair's extravagance. In a Channel 4 *Dispatches* film entitled *Politicians for Hire* (22 March 2010), to take another example, undercover reporters posing as lobbyists filmed a variety of British politicians – Sir John Butterfill, Stephen Byers, Patricia Hewitt, Geoff Hoon, Margaret Moran and Baroness Sally Morgan – offering to render their political services in support of the transport, pharmaceutical and supermarket industries. Some politicians offered to ask questions in the House of Commons without declaring their interests and requested large sums of money for their assistance. Intriguing as this exposé was, its political impact was not evenly felt: all but one of those implicated was a Labour politician, suiting the political interests of the soon-to-be-elected Conservative party. In the interests of balance here we might recall the scandals about sexual misconduct and 'cash-for-questions' involving Conservative MPs in the mid-1990s. In his book *What's Left?*, Nick Cohen argues that these journalistic exposés of 'sleaze' in the Major government disprove Chomsky and Herman's propaganda model of the media, showing that the news media is a fourth estate that crusades against abuses of power. But in fact the revelations of Conservative corruption helped to clear the way for the Labour Party's election in 1997 and thus illustrate very well the media's subordination to powerful interests.

Political scandals are common fare not only in hard news, but also in satirical entertainments such as BBC television's *Have I Got News for You?* and *Mock the Week* and BBC Radio 4's *The News Quiz*. Yet by emphasizing the greed and corruption of individual politicians or particular parliamentary parties, such programmes ultimately have a conservative function, promoting an ascendant faction of the ruling class over its rivals and obscuring how the state as a whole serves the interests of capitalism. While understandable, shock and outrage over media scandals are also easily co-opted for conservative ends. Therefore, as the anonymous authors of *The Coming Insurrection* advise, 'it's useless to *react* to the news of the day; instead we should understand each report as a manoeuvre in a hostile field of strategies to be decoded, operations designed to provoke a specific reaction'. To paraphrase Spinoza, we should not weep, but understand.

We should be wary, too, of claims that the media's propaganda function is significantly undermined by the development of new communications technologies. According to techno-progressivist myth, the Internet has broken down the stifling communicational hierarchies of the 'old media', creating unprecedented opportunities for democratic interchange. The World Wide Web has certainly been at the vanguard of what the cultural critic Mark

Poster terms the 'second media age' of user-generated content and rhizomatic, global interaction and its potential as a medium of 'horizontal' political communication is often excitedly hypothesized. Yet the assumption that these developments necessarily expand the scope for radical political action is eminently challengeable. Drawing on Lacan's notion of 'drive', Jodi Dean's book *Blog Culture* argues that the online 'activity' of the subject compulsively caught up in the 'affective networks' of the digital media is passivised and captured, in Lacan's words, 'in the circular movement of repeatedly missing its object'. Within the additive logic of what Dean calls 'communicative capitalism', each critique becomes just one more 'post' or update, no more or less salient than those it follows or precedes. Moreover, as Dean notes, the new digital media are exploited not only by radicals and progressives, but by all kinds of political groupings, including reactionaries – and, we might add, by the state itself. And even where the Internet does seem to have challenged capitalist power, the empire has retaliated. In 2010, Wikileaks disseminated secret military documents detailing the killing of civilians, assassination squads and cover-up attempts during the Iraq and Afghanistan wars. This suggests something of the Internet's potential to embarrass certain groups of politicians and expose media spin; yet Wikileaks faces an uncertain future following the arrest of its figurehead, Julian Assange, and the organisation has been subjected to financial and technical sabotage. In any case, the political implications of such leaks are not inherently radical: while Wikileaks has embarrassed Western capitalist states, its exposés have been welcomed – by many unpalatable anti-Western capitalist regimes.

Indeed, evidence for the Internet's radical potential is far from unambiguous. As Curran and Seaton comment in *Power Without Responsibility*, 'inequalities in the real world distort cyberspace, and limit its potential for improving society'. From its very beginnings as a decentralised US military communications network, the development of the Internet has been shaped by powerful forces. As advertisers shift their spending from the 'old' to the 'new' media and as the Internet is rapidly colonised by corporate interests (witness the takeover of MySpace in 2005 by Rupert Murdoch's News Corporation), the world of online opinion has increasingly come to reflect the capitalist worldview of the established media. This is clear not only from the rise of online advertising, but also from the nature of online news and political content. The most widely read online news sources are the websites of the BBC and other established media organisations. Meanwhile, the most popular news and current affairs blog sites, such as *The Guardian*'s Comment Is Free, are moderated by established media institutions and the most popular bloggers, as Matthew Hindman notes in *The Myth of Digital Democracy*, are journalists already known from their work in the 'old' media. Even in popular 'open source' online information resources, such as Wikipedia, political comment typically reproduces the hegemonic assumptions of the broadcast news media. Wikipedia's page about the foreign policy of the Clinton administration, for instance, asserts without irony that during his period in office, Clinton deployed US armed forces in order to 'end fighting, maintain peace, and protect innocent civilians'.

The Internet's potential to facilitate radical political praxis is also limited. As Gholam Khiabany and Annabelle Sreberny point out in *Blogistan*, the Iranian demonstrations in 2009 were mostly organised by word of mouth and text messages (although mobile networks were eventually blocked) rather than the Internet. This is hardly surprising since, as Evgeny Morozov notes in *The Net Delusion*, websites used for radical organisation are closely monitored by the state and are easily disrupted during periods of social upheaval: witness the suspension of the British site Fitwatch, which gave advice to students on avoiding surveillance by police Forward Intelligence Teams during the student fees protest in November 2010, or the suspension of Facebook services in Tunisia and Egypt during uprisings in those countries in January 2011. Moreover, while some web sites – such as libcom.org – are dedicated to the discussion of news and politics from a radical perspective, they are virtually invisible to those not already involved in radical political milieux.

Parliamentary parties, by contrast, enjoy considerable online visibility. In the run-up to the UK's 2010 general election, for instance, the Conservative party paid for Google advertisements that appeared when users searched for phrases such as 'hung parliament' – a prime example of what Hindman calls 'powerful hierarchies shaping a medium that continues to be celebrated for its openness'. On the day of the election itself, meanwhile, every British Facebook user was targeted with an 'election day message', reminding users that it was polling day and inviting them to click on a button to send the message 'I voted' to their friends. Along with the introduction of televised leaders' debates prior to the election, Facebook's drive to increase electoral partic- ipation may well have contributed to the relatively high turnout at the general election, which increased from 61% of those eligible to vote in 2005 to 65% in 2010. Similarly, in the US 2010 mid-term elections, Facebook helpfully provided users with an 'I voted' button, while the Democratic National Committee organised a YouTube broadcast in which Barack Obama asked voters to 'prove one more time that change comes from the bottom up'. Pro-Obama advertisements were also placed on social networking sites such as BlackPlanet.com. In a period when many workers, quite understandably, do not vote, it is unsurprising to find that new forms of 'social media' are increas- ingly being used to galvanise support for the electoral system and maintain public faith in liberal democracy.

Another form of new media, satellite television, may also appear to offer some potential relief from capitalist propaganda by making available foreign news channels that are critical of Western capitalist states. The news bulletins and discussion programmes broadcast by Iran's English-language television news channel Press TV, for example, include regular criticisms of the US, Britain and Israel, highlighting the military aggression of these states, the social problems faced by their populations and the suffering endured by victims of US, British and Israeli state terrorism. But despite these good offices, Press TV's news values are far from radical, since they reinforce the propaganda agenda of the Iranian clerical regime and exclude any discussion of the oppression of the Iranian working class. Moreover, Press TV counters Western Islamophobia not by invoking the radical ideal of human solidarity, but with a proliferation of news items about corrupt Jewish businessmen and rabbis whose cumulative effect is grossly anti-Semitic. The channel thus offers an alternative to Western media propaganda; yet it articulates capitalist ideology just as surely as its Western counterparts, substituting one set of scapegoats and bogeymen for another.

At this point, one may be tempted to remark resignedly that the capitalist media, for all their faults, at least 'give the people what they want'. The argument here is deceptively simple: if there were no demand for capitalist content, then the media would not supply it. This is quite true as far as it goes; but it ignores the fact that the media – and the ruling class in general – create and shape consumer demand *in the first place*. Writing about the US news media in his book *The Culture Struggle*, Michael Parenti gives an example, drawn from his own experience, of a small library

...that claimed to have no funds to acquire politically dissident titles but was well stocked with all sorts of media-hyped potboilers, and did manage to procure seven copies of Colin Powell's autobiography. This is not just a matter of supply responding to demand. Where did the demand to read about Powell come from? The media blitz that helped legit-imize the Gulf War of 1991 also catapulted its top military commander into the national limelight and made him an overnight superstar. It was media supply *creating* demand.

Public demand for media content is not formed in a vacuum, then, but is itself mediated. Parenti goes on to note that 'libraries and bookstores, not to mention newsstands and drugstores, are more likely to stock *Time* and *Newsweek* than such dissident publications as *Z Magazine* and *Dollars and Sense*'; since the public is seldom exposed to the radical ideas contained in the latter publications, it is hardly surprising that its demand for radical publications is modest.

Another common objection to 'propaganda model' of the media is that audiences do not believe everything they are shown and told. This, thankfully, is quite true. Audiences often read media texts 'against the grain', negotiating, resisting or even opposing the meanings of media texts. Acknowledging these strategies can help to guard against the dangers of textual determinism or 'internalism', wherein meaning is held to inhere solely within texts. Yet the extent of such critical readerly practices must not be overstated. The exaltation of the 'active audience theory' within cultural studies in the 1990s – a decade that constituted, ironically, one of lowest periods of class struggle activity in the capitalist era – was accompanied by a widespread rejection of the notion of 'false consciousness', which came to be seen as an expression of pessimistic elitism. This is unfortunate in some ways. As Steven Lukes proposes in *Power: A Radical View*:

'False consciousness' is a term that carries a heavy weight of unwelcome historical baggage. But that weight can be removed if one understands it to refer, not to the arrogant assertion of a privileged access to *truths* presumed unavailable to others, but rather to a cognitive power of considerable significance and scope: namely, the power to *mislead*.

Contrary to the Panglossian perspective of many active audience theorists, the media's power to mislead is enormous: research conducted by the Glasgow Media Group, for instance, showed significant correlations between the biased media reporting of the Miners' Strike and the Israeli-Palestinian conflict and public beliefs about those topics, suggesting that the notion of false consciousness, or something like it, remains relevant for media criticism. While media audiences are certainly 'active' in many ways, the exclusion of radical perspectives from today's news and current affairs media drastically delimits the possibilities for turning this activity towards any form of ideological contestation.

12

Conclusion: politics and media studies beyond the left

These people of the Left party [...] might in reality be just as unimportant, but the composure of their bearing made them appear of more consequence – Franz Kafka, *The Trial*

Early in Franz Kafka's novel *The Trial*, the beleaguered hero Josef K. finds himself in a meeting hall surrounded by a crowd composed of two factions, before which he protests against the injustice of his unexplained arrest. As the epigraph above indicates, K. initially senses that the Left party is the more serious of these factions, and that its members are somehow sympathetic to his plight; but he shortly comes to the bitter realisation that 'they were all colleagues, these ostensible parties of the Right and the Left'. K.'s epiphany offers a warning to those who may be tempted to indulge in the narcissism of small differences – to proclaim that liberalism, for all its faults, is at least preferable to conservatism – for it can be argued that liberal political administrations are often just as oppressive as those of the right. Perry Anderson has argued in relation to America, for example, that the Nixon regime so despised by left-wing intellectuals was actually more progressive in domestic policy terms than that of the liberal Clinton.

More recently, many of the left-liberal academics who reviled the Republican president George W. Bush warmly welcomed Bush's supposedly 'progressive' Democratic successor Barack Obama. Their effusions were echoed in the liberal media. In a 2009 advertisement for the BBC News channel, for example, a handsome young new father holds a newborn baby in his arms

107

and watches the election of the new president on the television as a tender smile spreads across his face. Yet as communists argued all along, the election of Obama in 2008 represented political and ideological continuity with the Bush years, rather than change or a renewal of 'hope', the Obama campaign's watery buzzword. As Vaneigem famously observed, hope is the leash of submission. The Obama administration proved to be an even more deadly enemy of the working class than its forerunner, driving through a so-called healthcare 'reform' that required tens of millions of working class Americans to take out private insurance while boosting profits for the insurance and pharmaceutical industries; as even the liberal filmmaker Michael Moore has pointed out, the reform was a 'victory for capitalism'. Overseas, meanwhile, the Obama administration intensified conflict in the Middle East by bombing Pakistan, enormously increased troop numbers in Afghanistan, invaded Haiti after a devastating earthquake in that country, and vetoed a UN Security Council resolution on ending Israeli settlement expansion – all of which lends a truly Orwellian quality to the award of the 2009 Nobel Peace Prize to Obama. The *Washington Post* (5 June 2010) reported a dramatic increase in Special Operations under the Obama administration, while in his 2010 article 'The Iranian threat', Chomsky noted that the Obama administration had accelerated its predecessors' plans to acquire heavy ordnance, citing academic Dan Plesch's view that the US is 'gearing up totally for the destruction of Iran'.

A leader article published in *The Guardian* (5 June 2008) before Obama's election victory expressed the hope that Obama would 'use US power more wisely and effectively than Mr Bush for the world's urgent causes'. Yet if 'urgent causes' have been pursued by the Obama regime, they have been those of the US ruling class. Like the election of the black president David Palmer in Fox's television drama *24*, the election of Obama captivated liberal fantasy; no doubt the feminist left will hail the election of the first female US president – a scenario already anticipated in television dramas such as *Commander in Chief* – as an equally 'historic' and politically progressive moment. Yet all of this is window dressing: neither the racial identity, nor the personal charisma, nor the gender of a president alters her institutional status or the capitalist nature of her political attachments.

The progressive posturing of the British political left is no less hollow. At the time of writing in 2011, a Conservative and Liberal Democrat coalition is in power and implementing drastic cuts to working class living standards, while leftist elements including the Labour Party, the Trotskyists and the unions present themselves as the progressive alternative, or at least as the 'lesser evil', just as they did in the mid-1990s. But we should not be fooled again. Whatever the claims of the Labour Party, *The Guardian* or *New Statesman*, Labour's rule from 1997 until 2010 was characterised by massive imperialist violence abroad and deepened economic inequality at home. Nor does the official far left offer any alternative to these depredations. The state capitalist Socialist Workers Party (International Socialist Organization in the US), for example, seeks to impose socialism 'from above' by taking over the state in the name of the working class. In its supposedly 'progressive' support for small imperialist states over larger ones, it has endorsed a veritable roll call of third world butchers and oppressive regimes. Yet despite all of this, the parties of the left and far left collectively command a significant following among British workers.

Although conservative pundits may be wheeled on to media debates to enliven proceedings with daring defences of sexism or Islamophobia, generating ersatz controversy, a leftist consensus also dominates Britain's cultural life. Indeed, one can even partially agree with conservative critics, such as Robin Aitken, that the BBC is biased towards the left. Therein, indeed, lies the liberal media's importance for the state. Britain's ruling class is amongst the most experienced and sophisticated in the world and its operations are increasingly justified not by appeals to crude jingoism but to humanitarianism, human rights, feminism, anti-fascism and anti-imperialism – that is, to the liberal discourses propounded by the BBC, *The Guardian* and *New Statesman*.

We began this book by quoting one of capitalism's ur-propagandists, Edward Bernays. Bernays was a master of corporate and state propaganda whose PR strategies anticipated those of today's opinion makers. His propaganda campaign for the United Fruit Company led directly to the US Central Intelligence Agency's overthrow of the Guatemalan government. United Fruit used inexpensive labour in Central America in order to produce cheap bananas for the US market. When the Guatemalan government tried to curtail the company's power in the 1950s, Bernays exploited McCarthyist sentiment in the US, placing articles discussing the growing influence of Guatemala's 'Communists' in news and current affairs publications, from the *New York Times* to *Newsweek*. Crucially, Bernays – himself a liberal – recognised the importance of influencing the liberal media. As Larry Tye writes in his book about Bernays, *Father of Spin*, 'the fact that liberal journals like the *Nation* were [...] coming around was especially satisfying to Bernays, who believed that winning the liberals over was essential'. The same belief was shared by an ideologist of a different stripe, the Nazi propagandist Joseph Goebbels, who, as Nicholas Pronay notes in *Propaganda, Politics and Film, 1918-1945*, was excited by the BBC's ability to maintain the trust of the British public and to have secured a worldwide reputation for the British media as 'honest, free and truthful'. Goebbels understood that this made the BBC the perfect propaganda vehicle. Today, as then, the left-liberal media act not as a foil to capitalism, but as its last ditch defence, preventing those who reject conservative political positions from accessing or developing radical ideas.

In fact, right- and left-wing media can be argued to work not in opposition to each other, but in tandem. The essential continuity of the left and right wings of the news media is indicated by the ease with which some journalists are able to move between them. Joshua Rozenberg, for example, left the *Daily Telegraph* to become a well-known BBC legal correspondent, while John Kampfner moved from the reactionary *Daily Express* to become editor of *New Statesman* and a prominent liberal commentator. Both journalists at one time traded in populist conservatism, attacking, *inter alia*, Britain's supposed 'compensation culture'; yet both are now doyens of the British liberal media establishment. Indeed, whether consciously or not, journalists often appreciate far better than many 'radical' critics that both the left- and right-wing media are in the business of circulating capitalist propaganda. In this sense, as Al Franken once quipped, asking whether 'the media has a left- or right-wing, or a liberal or a conservative bias, is like asking if the problem with Al-Qaeda is [that] they use too much oil in their hummus'.

Adolf Hitler, in *Mein Kampf*, advised that effective propaganda must consist of slogans that 'should be persistently repeated until the very last individual has come to grasp the idea that has been put forward'. This book has outlined some of the contemporary applications of this prescription in a way that suggests a fundamental continuity between contemporary liberal democratic propaganda and earlier twentieth-century forms of capitalist propaganda, whether fascist or Stalinist. The notions that we must all 'do our bit' to save the environment, that strikes are acts of intransigence against the national interest, that 'our' state's imperialist slaughters are justified and that those of our enemies are genocides, that wage labour is necessary and ennobling, that liberal capitalism is the only viable political system, and that immigrants must be either exploited or deported – these notions are all 'persistently repeated' in today's 'democratic' news and current affairs media such that many people have come to accept them unquestioningly.

Yet the media cannot bear all of the blame for this state of affairs. As I have hinted throughout this book, academic critics of the media and cultural industries also play a part in maintaining illusions in liberal democracy. A left-liberal hegemony holds sway in British media and cultural studies, characterised by a commitment to 'radical democracy', opposition to neoliberalism in the name of state capitalism, the endorsement of supposedly 'progressive' capitalist politicians such as Jon Cruddas and Caroline Lucas and the rejection of revolutionary class struggle. A profound influence upon this milieu has been Ernesto Laclau and Chantal Mouffe's *Hegemony and Socialist Strategy*, which rejects the working class 'essentialism' of Marxist politics in favour of cross-class united front politics aimed at extending the supposedly growing freedoms of liberal democracy within the parliamentary structure. For the epigones of Laclau and Mouffe, the era of communist class struggle is over. Yet while today's hegemony theorists talk vaguely of the need for a 'new' politics, their strategies tend to result, as Ellen Meiksins Wood argues in *The Retreat from Class*, in classical liberal pluralism. Moreover, reports of the death of revolutionary politics are greatly exaggerated. In her piece 'The Communist Hypothesis', Jodi Dean points out that the viability of communism is perceived far more acutely by the right than by the left: why else, asks Dean, are conservatives so frequently moved to denounce it? Nor is the resurgence of communism merely a matter of perception: recently, membership of class struggle anarchist and left communist groups in the UK has been slowly growing. As Michael Burawoy noted over a decade ago in his article 'Marxism after Communism', Marxism 'has a boomerang-like character – the further you throw it, the more resilient its return'. Many workers are coming to realise that Marxism, as Sartre wrote half a century ago in *Search for a Method*, remains 'the philosophy of our time. We cannot go beyond it because we have not gone beyond the circumstances which engendered it'.

Contra the Laclauian hegemony theorists, it is not communism, but liberal democracy that can no longer be used for radical or even progressive ends. As the early twentieth century revolutionaries recognised, the outbreak of the First World War effectively marked the end of the era of evolutionary capitalist expansion and parliamentary progressivism. Moreover, as Luxemburg reminded Bernstein at that time, parliamentarism is not a more cautious means to the same end of social emancipation, but a different end, since the capitalist state cannot be used to achieve socialism 'from above'. Today, when the bankruptcy of parliamentarism is far more evident than it was a century ago, radicals can entertain no illusions about social democracy. Concomitantly, in the sphere of media criticism, the radical task is not to 'work with' the media industries and their regulatory bodies in order to campaign for 'better' media representations of the working class, or to defend so-called 'public service' media organisations against the encroachments of the market, but – through what Marx called 'ruthless criticism' – to expose the ruses of capitalism's representational apparatuses until such time as they can be overthrown. Here we might recall Karl Korsch's stipulation that Marxism is a critical method, not a positive one. Relevant too is Gáspár Tamás's distinction between 'Rousseauian socialism' and its Marxian counterpart: the former seeks to ameliorate the representation of the working class, the latter to abolish the class system altogether.

Under a capitalist system, the media industries will tend overwhelmingly to disseminate capitalist propaganda, whether in its rightist or leftist guise; only a radical change in social relations can change this state of affairs. The question is whether such a change can now be brought about. Just as it had a beginning, capitalism will certainly reach its end – the only question is *how*. On a global scale, the social problems which the development of capitalism has both produced and, paradoxically, enabled humanity to prevent – poverty, starvation, warfare and ecological disintegration – are worsening, indicating that the global class struggle may end with the breakdown of capitalist society and what Marx and Engels, in a pessimistic moment, called 'the mutual ruination of the contending classes'. The ruling class may yet be able to unleash a third world war, which, if fought with nuclear weapons, could bring about the end of the human species. Another possibility is that the international working class can overthrow the senescent system of capitalism and create a society based on human need rather than the profit of a ruling elite. The material conditions for such a transformation are now in place. In a 1975 interview, the council communist Paul Mattick noted that 'it is precisely the more advanced form of capitalism, with its advanced technology, high productivity, and network of communication, which offers a material base for the establishment of communism'. Even if this material base is daily being eroded by environmental decay, communism remains a possibility today. While certain historical forms, such as workers' councils, provide important models for proletarian organisation, there is no blueprint for achieving communism today and Marx himself refrained, wisely perhaps, from formulating 'recipes for the cook-shops of the future'. New revolutionary forms may yet emerge; but these will have nothing to do with the any of the capitalist political parties or the media apparatuses that support them. The struggle for communism requires us to reject both the anti-proletarian lies and slanders of the conservative right and the false alternatives offered by the left.

zero
books

Contemporary culture has eliminated both the concept of the public and the figure of the intellectual. Former public spaces – both physical and cultural – are now either derelict or colonized by advertising. A cretinous anti-intellectualism presides, cheerled by expensively educated hacks in the pay of multinational corporations who reassure their bored readers that there is no need to rouse themselves from their interpassive stupor. The informal censorship internalized and propagated by the cultural workers of late capitalism generates a banal conformity that the propaganda chiefs of Stalinism could only ever have dreamt of imposing. Zer0 Books knows that another kind of discourse – intellectual without being academic, popular without being populist – is not only possible: it is already flourishing, in the regions beyond the striplit malls of so-called mass media and the neurotically bureaucratic halls of the academy. Zer0 is committed to the idea of publishing as a making public of the intellectual. It is convinced that in the unthinking, blandly consensual culture in which we live, critical and engaged theoretical reflection is more important than ever before.